Hardcore Self Help: F**k Depression
By Robert Duff, Ph.D.

www.hardcoreselfhelp.com

Please direct all inquiries to duffthepsych@gmail.com

Disclaimer: This is a unique book. As you might be able to tell from the title, I am not afraid to be a little colorful with my language. If that bothers you, maybe try a more straight-laced self-help book. This book is intended for mature audiences. If you are a parent buying this for your teen, I encourage you to check out the book for yourself and then decide whether it would be appropriate for them.

This is the second book in the Hardcore Self Help book series. This book is a bit longer than the first. In F**k Anxiety, I wanted you to power through the book as fast as possible and then get out there to make some positive changes. F**k Depression is a bit less rushed. I use the same tone in which I talk directly to you like a friend, but I took my time to cover each area more fully.

Throughout the book, I give you a few different resources that you can use in your quest to overcome depression. Many of these are also available in printable form at duffthepsych.com/bookresources.

Table of Contents

Introduction

Depression fucking sucks. There's no other way to put it. It's a gross, heavy, disgusting monster that feels like a parasite that saps all of your life energy to sustain itself. If you are living with depression, you can probably admit you are in a vicious cycle. You want to crawl out of your depressed state, but most of the things that would possibly help just take too much energy and motivation, which you have none of because you are... well, depressed. Then you feel guilty about not doing those things that seem so easy for other people, which zaps you even more and drives you deeper into depression. It's bullshit and I understand that it probably makes you feel pretty frustrated.

That's okay. Right now, you don't need to feel confident or hopeful. I will be confident in you right now and you can pick up the reigns later. I know that you can get through this. My confidence in you is not misplaced or unfounded. You're fucking brilliant and I hope you give me the chance to prove it to you. Consider this: you are exhausted, right? Feeling like every single thing you do takes 1000% more effort because you have this annoying personal black cloud over your head as well as a backpack full of 100 heavy ass bricks that you carry around all day? There is no reason you should have picked up this book. Reading isn't all that fun and you've already learned that mostly anything you try to do to get better is pretty much useless. Here's the thing. You did it anyway. That's fucking huge.

I'm so proud of you for taking this chance. Stop shaking your head! It's a big deal and I am going to force feed you this compliment whether you like it or not. There is a piece of you that is still fighting this and I want to add a spark to that little ember and help you create a roaring fire of depression slaying badassery. You may feel numb and zombie-like, but you have not given up. We are still in this, friend. Let's get you back on track.

In the following chapters, I will teach you a bit about depression in real-person language. Let me pause here and introduce myself. My name is Robert Duff. I am a psychologist from Southern California. My goal with the Hardcore Self Help book series is to take the information that I have learned in my clinical work and in my Ph.D. education in psychology and translate it into straightforward language. In the field of psychology, there is this stupid tendency to make things way too complicated. In my opinion, you should be able to explain something simply if you truly understand it. That's what I do here. This is self-help for people who usually don't like self-help.

In my work as a psychologist I have had the honor of seeing real people just like you claw their way out of some really dark spots, and I would like to share some of the lessons and insights that helped them do that. Depression sucks hard, but it is not a death sentence. You are ready to move on. So let's get your ass movin'!

Ch. 1 Are You Actually Depressed?

Alright, so, many of you are probably not sure whether or not the crappy feelings you are having qualify as depression. We tend to throw around the term depression pretty casually here in the USA. You might hear someone say that they are depressed when their sports team blows it or when their favorite musical group loses a member. This points to one of the annoying things about depression: it is an emotion and it is also the name of a disorder. What I mean is, you can feel depressed without having *depression*. Throw in the fact that depression does not look the same for everyone and this shit can get really confusing. Let me try to clear it up a bit.

Have you ever lost a family member or favorite pet? Have you ever completely bombed a test that you needed to do well on in order to get the grade you wanted in a class? Have you broken up with a significant other? I could keep going, but what I am trying to get at is the fact that we have all encountered periods of sadness in our lives. What is distinct about the sadness that follows these sorts of events is that it is "reactional" in nature. That means you have gone through some shit and your heart is really heavy as a result. You might even have been more than "just a little sad". Maybe you were having a hard time eating, crying almost constantly, and feeling completely drained of your energy. It is common for difficult circumstances to throw you into a sort of temporary depression. This is a good thing. It means that you are a good human and that you cared about the issue in the first place. We run into trouble when our overwhelming feelings of sadness extend beyond the immediate situation. If the situation resolves and you still find yourself in the throes of these feelings, you might need to take a step back and evaluate whether you might be depressed.

Of course, many of you are probably here because you are in a similar emotional state, seemingly for no reason. Nobody died, and objectively things are not all that bad, but you just can't seem to stop feeling like garbage. In fact, that probably fuels the depressive fire even more. That knowledge that things could be worse. Depending on your circumstances and who you ask, there very well may be a reason for this depressed state you find yourself in ... it just might take some digging to find it. Even if you feel you have no reason to be in such bad shape, it is important to be honest with yourself and consider the possibility that something clinically significant might be going on here.

And we can't neglect to mention the people who have an easily identifiable reason for their depression. Trauma, abusive relationships, extreme poverty, a never ending series of tragedies... all of these things are damn good reasons to feel depressed. It's tough because these circumstances are not really "your fault". I want to stress to you that whether your depression has a clear origin or is more of a mystery, you can definitely find something useful in the contents of this book.

In the field of psychology, we use a book called the Diagnostic and Statistical Manual of Mental Disorders (DSM) to aid in determining whether issues meet criteria for a well-known psychological issue. The DSM is one of several different standard texts that are used to diagnose mental illness. Depression is such a common issue that any definition you find will be relatively similar. These are the current DSM criteria for a major depressive episode. You need to have five or more of these symptoms that occur during the same two-week period and represent a change from previous functioning. At least one of your symptoms has to be depressed mood or loss of interest or pleasure:

- Depressed mood for most of the day, nearly every day. In children or adolescents this can look more like irritable mood.

- Lowered interest or pleasure in nearly all activities for most of the day, nearly every day.

- Significant weight loss or weight gain (change in 5% of body weight in a month) when you haven't been intentionally changing your diet or a decrease in appetite, nearly every day.

- Insomnia (not sleeping enough) or hypersomnia (sleeping way too much), nearly every day.

- Either speeding (agitation) up or slowing (retardation) down of your activities, as noticed by other people.

- Fatigue or loss of energy, nearly every day.

- Feelings of worthlessness or over-the-top guilt, nearly every day.

- Trouble with thinking or concentrating, or indecisiveness, nearly every day.

- Recurrent thoughts of death, recurrent suicidal thoughts without a particular plan, a suicide attempt, or a specific plan for committing suicide.

For your experience to qualify as a major depressive episode, these symptoms need to be disrupting some important area of functioning such as your ability to operate socially or work effectively at school or your job. These symptoms also can't be due to the effects of drugs, medicine, or a medical condition. Certain medications can have a depressant effect, which is definitely a valid experience, but it is considered to be separate from a major depressive episode. I should back up for a moment and clarify why I keep saying "depressive episode". A huge number of people have a major depressive episode at some point in their lives. This is at least a two week period in which you meet those criteria that we just talked about. A smaller, but still way too large number of people experience major depressive disorder, which means that they have a pattern of recurrent depressive episodes across a portion of their lifetime. You can think of it as being similar to an eating disorder. You can have an episode of starving yourself, but that does not necessarily make you meet criteria for anorexia. It is the recurrent behavior over time that qualifies it as a psychological disorder.

Now I should talk a little bit about the fact that depression is not the same for everyone. It is difficult to stick to the books and convey what I'm trying to say about this, so please forgive me if I draw a bit more from personal experience than research here. One of the things that persistently pisses depressed people off is when they meet a mental health professional who instantly groups them into a very specific category in their mind. I'll be totally clear that not every mental health provider does this, but there are certainly enough dumbasses out there that do. I can totally understand why it is infuriating to feel like you are put into a box before you even get the chance to explain yourself. Sure, you have depression, but that doesn't mean that your depression is exactly the same as everyone else's. You are more than just a checklist of symptoms, and it can be really hard to deal with people who think that your depression is the over-the-top emotional, ugly crying, arrow-to-the-heart kind of depression when, in reality, you are having more of the annoyed at everyone, angry at self, agitated sort of depression. Those are two very different flavors. Let's talk about some of the unique ways that depression can manifest. Clearly, I won't be able to capture every single one of you unique snowflakes here, but maybe you identify with one of these.

Perhaps one of the more stereotypical versions of depression is what I like to call the "sorrowful" subtype. This one looks a lot like active grief. The way I can typically identify

9

someone in this mode is by asking whether they find themselves crying at literally everything. The wrong commercial comes on, you hear a song that makes you feel all the feels, the wind changes... you hardly need an excuse to shed some tears. It's like you're on the verge of breaking down 24/7. This version of depression really sucks because it's not exactly the type that you can hide easily. Not so awesome when you are trying to hold it together at work. You're just so fucking sad that it almost literally aches in your heart. Often people start off with this type of depression and progress from there. When you first feel the bitter sting of depression and start to question whether this is just who you are now, it can be startling and incredibly painful.

Sometimes people are depressed, but nobody notices. That's because they don't follow the archetype that I described above. Not to be stereotypical, but in the US a lot of guys seem to fall under this umbrella. Instead of becoming sorrowful, crying, and feeling that palpable heartache, some people instead look more angry or agitated. People who are in this mode tend to feel annoyed as hell at just about everything. Someone cut you off of the freeway? Pissed. Bad service at Starbucks? Irritated. Distant relative posting ignorant political garbage on Facebook? Fucking forget about it. Now there are some people that have a low tolerance for bullshit throughout their entire life. That's not what I'm talking about here. I'm talking about a distinct change that takes hold. Sure, all of those things are annoying in and of themselves, but that's not really what this is about. You are mad at yourself and nearly everything in the world just serves as a reminder of that. It's like a mirror that you are trying really hard to avoid looking into.

Both of the examples that I have mentioned are pretty easy to identify by their distinct behaviors. Another unique depressive presentation I have seen is the anhedonic type. Anhedonia literally means "without pleasure." In this type of depression, you don't feel much of anything. No matter if the things you encounter are extremely happy or entirely sad, you feel emotionally vacant. It's almost as if you have no emotional energy left to give, and all that is left is this hollow feeling in your chest. The numbness should feel sad, but you just can't quite bring yourself around to feeling sad. Typically, it is quite hard to identify what is wrong when you have this style of depression. You can't exactly put your finger on it, but it just doesn't feel right. You are there, but you aren't really there. Some people will turn to self-harm or extreme behaviors in this type of depression because they just want to feel a little bit of anything.

The last flavor of depression is the physically wrecked version. This is the type where you seem to internalize all of your depression. You know Kirby? The pink marshmallow videogame character? Imagine him sucking up a bomb and swallowing it. That bomb is your depression. Sometimes, it can feel like all your sadness expresses itself through your physical body. Common complaints are constantly feeling weak, sick, and tired. Exhaustion probably plays a big role in your life. You might turn down many opportunities that could be helpful simply because the mere thought of doing anything makes every muscle in your body cry. Perhaps you are legitimately sick more often than other people, but it's more than that. Things just seem to hit you harder than they should. This type is really hard. Maybe you have even gone to doctors and specialists to try to figure out what's wrong and no matter what tests they give, they can't find anything in particular that should be making you feel this way. (Now, I should clarify that this sort of depression is not the same thing as having a chronic fatigue disorder or autoimmune problems. Those can cause a lot of strange and confusing physical issues. The defining factor that would help you know that this is depression would be that it ebbs and flows depending on your emotional state. If you were feeling great physically when you were happy and things seemed pretty good in your life and once things took a turn, your body started breaking down, you might be looking at depression.)

Again, this is not mutually exclusive with physical problems. I write more about physical issues that can *look* like depression later on, so definitely have a look there as well.

Like I said, those are just a few of the "types" of depression I've encountered. It is not meant to be an exhaustive list. The point I am trying to get across is that depression is not one thing. Sure there are similarities in each type, but they're not identical. Think of it this way: not all dancers are the same. If you put a ballet dancer together with a break dancer, they may not feel like they are members of the same tribe. Sure they both dance, but the way in which they dance is pretty damn different. Of course they can find similarities between them and can certainly learn from one another. That's often how it is with depression. I see this all the time in support groups. If a group is dominated by one subtype of depression, there may be a new member who feels like they just can't relate. Just like those dancers, they eventually are able to find some common ground and learn from one another. I tried to write this book in a way that could be helpful to all of you. (If you come to the end of the book and feel like your issues were not addressed, please let me know so I can do better in the future.)

So take a nice long look at yourself. Review the symptoms and depressive presentations that I have talked about so far. Do these line up with your experience? I have to say you really should leave definitive diagnosis to professionals who have the chance to meet you in person. Our generation has this really bad habit of using WebMD and self-diagnosing... don't pretend like you have never done it. The point of recognizing your symptoms and identifying the potential of a disorder is that you can take that information with you when you seek professional diagnosis. You don't have to have a diagnosable psychiatric issue to benefit from the knowledge bombs I drop on you in this book. These tips can help anyone who deals with depressive symptoms regardless of whether they get to join the exclusive "officially depressed" club or not.

Before we move on to the next sections of this book where we will break down some of the different issues that are present in depression and talk about ways to fight back against them, I want to dive a little bit deeper into defining depression. If you already get the picture and want to skip ahead, please do, but I know there are some of you out there that will kill me if I don't at least mention some of the other disorders that are related to depression, but are unique beasts in their own right. Diagnostically speaking, major depression is in a category of issues called "mood disorders". Let's talk about a few other ones.

You have probably heard of bipolar disorder right? It used to be called manic-depressive disorder because it is characterized by two different states: mania and depression. Depression you already know about, since you have been paying close attention and taking vigorous notes throughout this chapter. Mania is the flip side of the coin. Instead of feeling down in the dumps, you feel like a superhero. Someone with mania will often experience a great surge in energy that leads them to go for long periods without sleeping. They might rapidly start new projects and be overly productive. There is this sense of euphoria that is often marked by delusional thinking. By that I mean that the person who is in a manic phase will often have unrealistic thinking such as, "I have the best idea for a new company. It's like Uber for drug dealers. I need to sell my house and move to Silicon Valley because that's where tech startups live. Time to start researching plane tickets and places to list my house for immediate sale." There are different types of bipolar and some nuances to diagnosing it, which I will not get into here, but essentially someone with bipolar goes through distinct periods of depression and that mania that I described. Both of the "poles" of this disorder can be devastating. It is hard to treat as well, because regardless of the danger, it can feel fucking awesome to be manic. Even though you might be wrecking your body, making poor decisions, and freaking everybody out... beats the hell out of depression right? At least that's what it feels like. In reality, mania can be even more dangerous than depression because you are more likely to actually get off your ass and do something that you are going to regret later. If you are in the bipolar camp, you can certainly learn a few things from this book, but I would urge you to pay particular attention to the chapter about getting professional help.

Another one to mention is persistent depressive disorder, which used to be known as dysthymic disorder. That is where you don't tend to go into full blown depressive episodes, but you continuously have a low-grade depression that just never seems to lift.

Then you have seasonal affective disorder, which is basically depression that is only expressed during certain seasons. Most often this shift in mood occurs during the more dreary winter months. Mothers can also have postpartum depression, which is when "baby blues" following the birth of a new little one continue to be strong and persistent after a few weeks. It is often still a temporary issue, but it can transition into major depression if left unchecked.

Okay, that's about all I want to dive into right now. I think it's important to arm yourself with some knowledge about the different symptoms that you might be experiencing, but I know this chapter was also kind of a bummer. On one hand, you might recognize that you are not alone in your struggle. On the other, realizing that you are depressed can be... well... fucking depressing. That's okay. Depression sucks because it is a "sticky" problem that can be really hard to shake on your own, but there is actually a lot that can be done to facilitate the process. You have taken the first step toward kicking these issues by reading this far. Give yourself a nice little pat on the back. In the rest of the book, I will talk about specific issues that are often encountered in depression and give my thoughts about how you can work around them. We will cover things like motivation, thinking patterns, ways to set yourself up for success, and finding professional help. Let's get into it!

Ch. 2 Getting the Ball Rolling

So this is ironic. I am having the hardest time finding the motivation and desire to write this chapter. I mean, I want to have the desire to write it, but I have tried a bunch of times to bring myself to actually start writing and have failed. Well, when I say that "tried", I guess I mean that I have sat there and waited to feel motivated enough to start writing. Of course, that is where I went wrong. I am not motivated right now, but I have already written 6 sentences. Swag. One of the superpowers that this evil villain named depression has is the ability to drain you of your energy and motivation. To make you feel hopeless and stuck. Often you are left trying to internally search for this feeling of motivation that you remember having at some point in your life, but that has not been present for quite some time. That is a trap. If you wait to feel motivated before you move forward with the things that you want or need to do, you will never do them. Low motivation and low energy are symptoms of depression, and they suck. Interestingly, one of the most effective forms of treatment for depression was invented by Nike. Okay, it wasn't actually invented by them, but they coined the tagline that I want you to remember: Just Do It.

In the world of psychology, we call this type of treatment for depression Behavioral Activation. Behavioral Activation acknowledges that when you are depressed, you fall into a negative behavioral pattern where you not only lose motivation to do the important stuff that you need to take care of, but you also stop doing the things that bring you happiness and pleasure. Basically, everything feels like it sucks, so what is the point of doing anything? I think of Behavioral Activation as the science of "duh" because you basically need to start doing the opposite. You need to push yourself to do things anyway even though you don't want to. Especially because you don't want to.

Have you felt anhedonia? This is that feeling that everything is just "meh." Cute picture of a cat wearing an ugly Christmas sweater? Meh. Top 10 laugh out loud clips on Youtube? Meh. Someone pays you a huge compliment, acknowledging the wonderful qualities that they appreciate about you as a person? Meh. Promotion at work? Meh. You get the idea. Everything just feels very bland and all of the things that used to have an effect on you basically fall flat. It is very common for people with depression to experience that feeling of anhedonia, which is separate from those more sharply painful feelings of sorrow, which can also be present. Awesomely, this can be undone. Essentially, you have learned to stop feeling pleasure, and you need to re-train your brain to recognize and benefit from the things that should be having a positive impact on you. How? You guessed it - Just Do It.

You are really going to have to take my word on this because, so far, this probably seems like the most obvious bullshit you have ever heard. If it was that simple, you would have already done it, right? Well, yes and no. You haven't done it because it is really hard to claw yourself out of this stupid pit that you have fallen in. You need an action plan, and you need a kick in the ass. Let me be that kick in the ass. Let's do an exercise.

I want you to get out a piece of paper and write down 10-15 things that you used to provide you happiness, pleasure, motivation, laughter, or any other positive experience. Please do not write things that suck. I am sure that you used to do chores more often than you do now, but that's not the point of this list. If you write down "do laundry" or "finally clean the garage" I am going to stab you with a fork. I can't predict the exact things that make you happy, but you might write down things like "go to the movies", "take a walk", "play some video games", "read a book", "get the dog a new toy to play with", "invite a friend for lunch", "get a pedicure", "go surfing", "cook dinner for my kids", or "play some music". These are things that once felt great to you, but are currently falling flat. You need to reconnect to these things, and you need to re-train your brain to feel good about these things again. So, go ahead and make that list. If some emotion comes up for you while you are writing it, that is totally okay. It can be hard to recognize how many things have fallen by the wayside during the battle with depression.

Activities
1. Go to dinner with friends.
2. Get coffee.
3. Read book for fun.
4. Go to the movies.
5. Take a walk.
6. Get a mani/pedi.
7. Call mom.
8. Listen to favorite album.
9. Doodle for an hour.
10. Take a bath.

You have probably seen the cartoons where someone has an angel on one shoulder and a devil on the other, right? Well, depression is that devil that sits on your shoulder and whispers in your ear to tell you this exercise is useless. It will tell you that you don't deserve to do fun, pleasurable things for yourself. Especially when there are more important things that you are neglecting. If depression is going to be that devil, let me be the angel on the other shoulder telling that devil guy to shut the fuck up. Being stuck in the weeds does not mean that you don't deserve to take time to re-engage with these activities. We will most certainly get to the "important" stuff as well. This is just step one.

Alright, so back to the exercise. Once you write down those 10-15 things, I want you to think about two different variables. The first one is how much happiness, pleasure, reward, etc. you are likely to get from the activity. I'll give a few personal examples for my life. Going out to get some coffee would be pretty nice, but it's not necessarily going to be a top 10 of the month sort of activity. I'd rate it at about a 5 out of 10 on my reward scale. Playing some videogames for a couple hours might be more like a 6 or 7. Going out to a nice dinner and getting an expensive bottle of wine (provided the money is there) would be closer to an 8 or a 9. This is all very personal and subjective. Here's the thing: these ratings can shift depending on the context. If it is freezing out and I am tired as all hell, that pumpkin spice latte is suddenly going to be worth 8 points instead of 5. Why don't you go through and rate all of the activities that you listed on the same 0-10 scale, where 0 is nothing special and 10 is pee-your-pants exciting.

Activity	Reward		
Get coffee	5		
Dinner w/ friends	9		
Take a walk	8		
Listen to favorite album	4		

Great. Now that you have rated how rewarding each of those activities are, I want you to think about the second variable, which is the difficulty of the activity. Again, this is very personal to you and can change over time. If you are a seasoned runner and you haven't given up that activity despite your depression, running 2 miles might be very low on the difficulty chart. If you are just trying to get started with running, it will be much higher. Something a bit easier might be watching your favorite show on Netflix, which would be more like 2 out of 10 on the difficulty scale. Go back through your chart and add difficulty ratings to each of your activities that you listed on that 0-10 scale where 0 is something you could do in your sleep and 10 is your most herculean effort.

Activity	Reward	Difficulty	
Get coffee	5	3	
Dinner w/ friends	9	9	
Take a walk	8	3	
Listen to favorite album	4	1	

Awesome. So now, we have a nice little chart set up with a bunch of activities that your asshole depression has told you to stop caring about, and each item on that chart has a rating for reward and a rating for difficulty. We already know that your motivation has probably been obliterated through the depressive process, so what we need right now is an easy win.

Let's do a little math here. All I want you to do is subtract your difficulty from your reward. For instance, if getting coffee is a 5 in the reward column and a 3 in the difficulty column, you are left with a value of 2. Going to dinner with friends might be a 9 in terms of reward for you, but if it takes 9 units of effort, you are left with a value of 0. Your easy win is the activity that has the highest "win value" after performing that calculation. This is where you start.

Activity	Reward	Difficulty	Win Value
Get coffee	5	3	2
Dinner w/ friends	9	9	0
Take a walk	8	3	5
Listen to favorite album	4	1	3

A few things to keep in mind: Remember that this list of activities are things that you used to enjoy but have let slide since depression dug its stupid claws into you. That means that for me, I am not allowed to use playing video games as one of these activities. Even though I get a high value from it (7 reward - 2 difficulty = 5), it is something that I have not stopped doing. More of the same isn't what we are looking for here. I want you to shake things up. We are fighting against the pattern of sameness, not reinforcing it. The other thing to keep in mind is that this simple calculation is for finding your first easy wins. This does not mean that these are going to have the biggest impact on your mood and wellbeing in the long run. These are just the easiest places to start. Running a marathon is going to be off the charts in terms of difficulty, but it might also be off the charts in personal meaning and change your life forever, if you can get yourself to that point. For now, we want to start simple and break the cycle of negative actions leading to negative emotions.

Okay, so all of that is well and good, and you might even be feeling pretty motivated right now to get out there and kick ass with your first easy win. That motivation will not last forever, though. As soon as you put down this book for the day, the emotional high from being here with me and inspiring yourself by planning to destroy your depression will slowly fade away. There is nothing wrong with that. It's totally normal to have peaks in your motivation, and inspiration that don't last forever. What you need to do is capitalize on your motivation in this moment to set yourself up for success later. One way you can do that is by making more concrete plans to follow through with your first easy wins. Even though I am calling them easy, they are sometimes very hard when you are first starting the depression exterminating process. Therefore, if you simply say to yourself, "Alright, I will go and take a walk tomorrow," you just might skip that walk. However, if you go on your phone and say, "Remind me to go for a walk tomorrow at 2 pm," you might be a little more likely to follow through. Be specific and be reasonable. Say going to the gym is on your list because you used to be pretty ripped and enjoyed lifting several times per week. Starting off with one specific time next week to go and lift might be much more feasible at this point in time than saying you'll go three times per week starting today. Going too hard right away will just turn you off and make you feel bad about yourself.

Getting started is often the hardest part, so I have a few tips to get you moving, even when motivation is lacking. The first is called the 5-minute rule, and it is just like it sounds. You can handle just about anything for at least 5 minutes. When you use the 5-minute rule, you give yourself the option of bailing out from the activity you wanted to engage in, but only after at least 5 minutes of giving it a shot. So, if you start trying something out and after that time period, it is completely unbearable, then by all means call it quits and try another day. However, what you will often find is that once you get the ball rolling on an activity, it's really not as bad as you thought it would be, and the ball tends to keep rolling on its own. You just have to ignore that annoying ass voice in your head that tries to hold you back for long enough to get started on the damn thing. That whole saying of "fake it 'til you make it" actually has a lot of validity. Your jerk of a brain is so used to not having motivation and so used to not deriving pleasure from fun activities that you need to beat it back into shape. You don't *have* to be motivated to do things that normally take motivation. You just need to *act* as if you were motivated. I can ask myself, "What would Robert do if he *was* motivated right now?" That gives you the goal to press toward. Do the damn thing and I promise you that the feelings will start to catch up. If you are having trouble playing that part, regardless of your pre-planning and psyching yourself up, maybe you should enlist some help. If you are the type of person to be fine letting yourself down, but almost never fail to keep commitments with others, you might want to schedule your walk or trip to the bookstore with a friend who can help keep you accountable.

Activity scheduling seems to be most helpful when you can do it for your entire day. Don't worry. Some parts of the day will always be unpredictable, and you most likely won't stick to your schedule 100%, but when you are first getting started in this process of behavioral activation, it can be so valuable to literally schedule out every hour of your day. Schedule time to take breaks and be a lazy vegetable, but also schedule time to engage in those activities that you used to love. When you get to the end of your day, take a look at your schedule and notice what your emotional state was like during the different parts of the day. Maybe you had a peak in your happiness and motivation a few hours after lunch, and your personal black rain cloud was most apparent when you first woke up in the morning. You can use this information to your advantage. In that example, you would probably need the most support from your team to get your ass up and moving in the morning. On the other hand, you can trust that you will have the most motivation to do some solo depression ass kicking during the afternoon. Taking the time to notice and analyze your own patterns can serve as an amazing self-feedback tool that allows you to dial in the awesome work that you continue to put in and amplify the effects of this behavioral activation.

There are a million ways to skin this cat. The bottom line is you need to find the best way for you to start doing those things that you aren't doing. Start with the easy wins that we talked about and that should start to increase your baseline level of happiness and motivation. Don't forget that depression is a vicious cycle. Having no motivation and no energy is a symptom of depression, and taking no action is also something that makes you feel more depressed. This cycle keeps going around and around. When you start to break that cycle by *doing* things, your level of overall depression will start to decrease, which will have the side effect of increasing that reservoir of motivation that you have to spend. Create a positive snowball effect that will enable you to make the shift from re-engaging with pleasurable activities to re-engaging with activities that aren't always fun, but are necessary for living a meaningful life such as writing your paper, calling your mom to let her know that you are still alive, figuring out your finances, or cleaning your apartment.

I promise I'm not just pulling this stuff out of my ass. There is a physiological difference in the brains of people who have depression marked by low motivation and the stupid lucky people out there who don't have to contend with it. I want to talk about biology with you for a little bit. I'll try not to nerd out too hard and keep it straightforward, because it's important to have a basic understanding of neurobiology to understand just how it can feel so damn hard to get the ball rolling when you are depressed. So, the brain is full of these crazy cells called neurons. These cells carry electrical and chemical impulses throughout your brain and govern just about every aspect of your behavior. There are around 100 billion neurons in your brain, and they constantly communicate with one another through the use of these awesome little chemicals called neurotransmitters. Basically, one neuron produces a neurotransmitter and sends it floating over to another neuron. If that neuron has the right type of receptor and it's open for business at the time, it will accept the neurotransmitter like a puzzle piece. That will serve as a signal for that second neuron to take some sort of action.

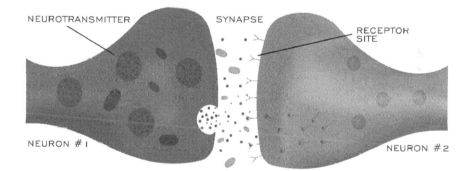

Now in depression, there isn't just one specific way that the brain changes. We are still in the process of understanding all of the neurochemical intricacies involved in individuals with depression (damn that sentence sounded smart). What we do know at the moment is that there are three main neurotransmitters involved when depression takes hold. Those neurotransmitters are serotonin, norepinephrine, and dopamine. You've probably heard of dopamine before. This is the neurotransmitter that makes you feel pleasure. Some people call it the "feel good molecule." Let me put it this way … a lot of "recreational" drugs act by providing a rush of dopamine that makes you feel awesome and rewards your behavior, which can eventually lead to addiction (we'll save that for another book). There are some really interesting things that happen with neurotransmitters that can make your brain all out of whack. Remember in that description above how there were two neurons: one sender and one receiver? The space between those two neurons is called the "synapse." When you take illegal drugs like cocaine, you artificially flood that synapse with dopamine. The result is that the receiving neuron (#2) goes, "Holy shit! I feel great, but we have WAY too much dopamine over here. HEY JOHN (neuron #1) YOU CAN STOP MAKING DOPAMINE. WE GOT TONS!" Your brain adapts quickly to changes like this to keep you in a lovely balanced homeostasis. That means that it will "down regulate" production of dopamine and will turn on those "closed for business" signs on the receptor sites of the receiving neuron. If you were to suddenly take away that drug, you brain would still be used to this new norm of not having to produce dopamine, and suddenly you have that anhedonia that we talked about. Everything feels like shit.

For depression that involves low motivation and lethargy, the outcome is basically the same, but the process is a little bit different. The second, receiving end, neuron will also turn on its "closed for business" sign if it doesn't get much dopamine knocking at its door. It's sort of like supply and demand. Think of it like a bar or a restaurant; if there are only a few patrons that come in throughout the week, the place is going to start reducing the hours it's open so that it doesn't lose so much money. If neuron #1 stops sending dopamine patrons to the pub over at neuron #2, they will start to close for business more often, and any dopamine that is produced may never result in making you feel happy. That, in turn, will make neuron #1 go, "Well screw that guy," and start sending less and less patrons over since they always end up coming back and saying, "Dude that place sucks. It wasn't even open when we went by." Friends. This is why everything feels so shitty. Your brain has just acquired a really bad habit of not making as much dopamine and also not even converting the dopamine to feelings of pleasure when it is generated.

This is a WAY overly simplistic description of how it works, but I hope it helps you understand a bit more about why it can be so hard to get the damn ball rolling in the middle of a depressive episode. You are literally fighting against your biology. That's the thing, though. Since you are a kickass human being, you do have the power to fight against your biology. You can say, "Hey asshole, I know that you've gotten used to the way things are, but it's time for you to start getting back into shape." You can literally retrain your brain to derive pleasure from things that used to feel awesome to you. Think of the bar example again. If neuron #1 suddenly starts sending a ton of patrons over to the pub at neuron #2, the doors will not reopen immediately. The owner of the pub will hear that they missed out on a ton of business and then maybe open up a few more days during the next week to see if the trend keeps up. If neuron #1 stays consistent and keeps sending people down to neuron #2 to get turnt (read: drunk), the owner of the pub will be inclined to stay open more and more often. So when you do activities that are fun and pleasurable, you will be sending dopamine into that synapse. Over time, by staying consistent and forcing yourself to do those activities that were once pleasurable for you, you can train your brain to start opening for business and feeling happiness again. Pretty fucking awesome, if you ask me. The coolest part is that once you develop your neural groove again, the happiness and pleasure will start to become more effortless. Things that you didn't even intend to make you happy will make you happy. That way, the random goat picture on twitter is no longer "meh" and is now "OMG I JUST GOAT SO HAPPY IN MY HEART!" (Side note: please go follow @TheSassyGoats on twitter for your daily dose of happy.)

I bet a lot of you asked yourselves earlier in the chapter how doing pleasurable, unimportant activities can eventually lead to you accomplishing the important stuff in your life. I understand the skepticism, but to use the bar example one last time, there is no point in the pub at neuron #2 suddenly converting to a high class, expensive mixology bar if they aren't getting any patrons on a daily basis. Once the demand is there, they have more wiggle room to take risks and put in more of their own effort into trying different things. In the same way, once you start this process of retraining your brain, you will have more overall motivation to work with. You can afford to expend some of it on activities that don't always feel awesome but are important to do. More importantly, sometimes tough activities like finishing your homework or cleaning the garage DO feel awesome. The result of you continually force-feeding your brain dopamine through pleasurable activities is that you may just open up enough receptors that the accomplishment of achieving your goals feels pretty kickass too. Maybe you can remember a time that this was the case. Getting a good grade on a project that was really difficult? Beating your personal record in some athletic activity? Finally getting your fingers to cooperate when trying to learn the guitar tabs to your favorite song? That shit feels amazing. Start with your easy wins and work toward the bigger stuff. You WILL get there.

At first, the process of retraining your brain and being productive again will feel grueling. It's like trying to get ripped again after an entire summer of pizza and Netflix. There is also the question of how hard to push. When I've described this approach, some people have expressed concern that they don't want to push so hard that they end up burning themselves out. For this concern, my advice would again be to enlist the support of others. Not only can you pick up on some of their contagious motivation and support, but they can also help serve as a gauge for you when you need to know whether you're really pushing yourself too hard or if it seems on track. A good rule of thumb is: if you are crashing really hard and feeling more depressed after you finish one of your activities, you may be pushing too hard and should probably start with something a little easier.

If you find that no matter how hard you try, you just cannot get the ball rolling, even on these easy wins, and you have already tried the strategies that I have outlined here, it may be useful to consider medication. I talk more about this in a later chapter, but the purpose of medication for depression is basically to give you a little boost in your neurotransmitters to ease your lethargy and low motivation a bit, so you have more emotional energy available and can put in the work re-training your brain like we talked about above. More on that later.

Ch. 3 Your Brain Is a Troll

I talked a lot about the ways in which your brain trolls you in my previous book, F**k Anxiety, but it is important to talk about them here too. They also play a huge role in depression. Having depression is like viewing the world through shit-colored glasses. Everything just has a different tint to it. Even the good stuff is hard to take seriously because you are filtering it through a 50 shades of crap. Let me do a little review of the way in which thoughts screw with us and how we can take some control back.

Let's continue with that glasses idea. When something happens in the world, whether it be to us directly or in general, we filter it through the lens of our thoughts and beliefs. This has a direct impact on the way we feel. The thing is, depression plays a lot of tricks on us, and we end up with distorted thinking patterns that tell us things like "you don't matter", "nothing you do is going to help", or "nobody likes you". Let's go through some examples together, so I can show you how thinking gets in the way of your emotional success. The following examples are taken from real feedback that I have gotten from those of you who were gracious enough to share your thoughts with me during the creation of this book. You rock.

Here is a thought pattern that some of you have probably fallen into: blaming yourself for everything. Even if something is logically outside your sphere of influence, you assume that somehow you have to be responsible for any mishap. In turn, you feel the need to apologize and beat yourself up emotionally. I don't mean something as obscure as seeing a plane crash on television and assuming that you somehow are to blame. Let's say that your significant other was up for a promotion at work and didn't end up getting it despite their confidence and hard work. Some healthy assumptions and beliefs about this situation might be that there was a better candidate for the promotion who really went above and beyond to seal the deal. Perhaps your mate's employer is in a tight spot financially and is trying everything that they can to avoid giving out more money, so they decided to skip this round of promotions entirely. When you filter the world through your shit-colored glasses, you instead just find a way to blame yourself for what happened. Maybe it is because you got into a fight a few nights ago, and it must have been distracting them and put them into a negative emotional state. Or maybe it is because you are too needy and took up all of their time they could have spent preparing for the interview, and they were unprepared as a result. Seeing it on paper might seem a bit ridiculous, but we totally do stuff like this.

Here's a super common one that can cause all sorts of problems: "Things never work out for me, so what's the point?" Hopelessness is a symptom of depression. That is a really important thing to remember. That is why you feel like you are never going to overcome your depression. That's what the depression devil is whispering in your ear all the time. Now, I'm not calling you dumb, but most of the time depressive hopelessness is not the result of logical reasoning. It's a trick that your mind plays on you to convince you that it's not worth trying. Let's say that you are trying to get more physical exercise to improve your physical and mental health. Well, when you think about it, there is really no point... last time you tried to exercise, it didn't make much difference, so why bother trying this time? This mental filter is causing you to not notice the fact that all of the positive effects of exercise are not evident right away, and you gave up last time pretty early into the process due to the very same cognitive trap that is playing out right now. This is one of the main challenges in writing a book like this. Trying to convince you that the voice in your head, the one that tells you there is no point in trying, is completely wrong.

I don't want you to be all rosy and blindly optimistic. That's just annoying. Instead, I want to encourage you to be more realistic. Be a good scientist. Before you jump to conclusions based on your gut feeling and the influence of the depression devil on your shoulder, give yourself the chance to examine the evidence. If it turns out that all of the objective evidence still points to something upsetting, then by all means be upset. Like I said earlier, shitty things should feel shitty. However, if you are experiencing depression, it is almost guaranteed that you are distorting the way in which you interpret the world to match gross feelings in your heart.

There are a few ways that we can counteract this process and bring about a healthier pattern of thinking. One big piece of advice I have is to avoid keeping it to yourself. If you have people in your life that you can talk to, tell them a bit about what you are struggling with internally. Help them understand your thought process and then invite their feedback about whether it makes sense. You should tell them that you aren't just looking to be told that everything will be okay, but rather that you want to know how they would think about this situation if it were happening to them. (I should interrupt here to mention that this works much better when you enlist the help of people who are not also depressed. Substituting one distorted thought process for another is not going to do much good.)

There are a couple barriers to asking people for their opinion of your thoughts. For some people, that will feel very exposing and scary. Opening up is not always easy and I think it is even scarier when you know deep down that your current thought process might be a bit skewed. No one likes to be thought of as crazy. If this is a barrier for you, it might be most useful to enlist the help of the top 1% of people in your life that you really trust and who you are almost certain will be there for you no matter what. If your life is an ever changing equation, these people are the constants. This is different for everyone. For some people, a parent provides that unconditional support. For others, they have a best friend from school who will always call you on your bullshit but never love you any less. Start with these people and recruit them as your logical barometers. Don't ask them whether you should be upset. Ask them if your line of thinking makes sense. Ask them how they would think about a given situation. There is no right or wrong here. You just want to get some alternative perspectives so you can really consider all sides of the evidence before you conclude that you truly deserve to feel like shit.

Another potential barrier is a lack of people in your environment that you can access. Luckily, technology like the Internet and texting has given us unprecedented access to friends and family whenever we may need them. Sometimes it just isn't possible or convenient to reach out to someone else, though. For those situations, I would encourage you to envision someone that you care about. As before, this can be a friend, family member, or miscellaneous loved one. Now, think about that person coming to you and describing a similar situation. What feedback would you have for them? This works exceptionally well with that "best friend who calls you on your bullshit" I mentioned earlier, because you can imagine yourself saying, "Dude, you're an idiot. That doesn't even make sense." What holes can you poke in their logic that might explain exactly why they feel so terrible about the situation at hand? Even better, you can combine these two approaches. You have some people in your life that serve as logical barometers for you. You reach out to them every so often and request feedback about your patterns of thinking. Over time, you start to internalize their voices and their thinking styles. So when the depression devil pops up on your shoulder and whispers some stupid self-sabotaging pseudo-logic in your ear, you also have your panel of trusted advisors that pop up and provide some alternative approaches that they would be more likely to employ. In the end, the decision about how to proceed is always yours, but using these strategies gives you the best shot at success. It's fairer and is one step in the direction of being less of a dick to yourself.

I also want to talk for a bit about a psychobabble term that you may have heard before. Have you ever heard of schemas? The word schema (skee - muh) basically just refers to your own unique pattern of thinking. It's how you selectively pay attention to certain things while ignoring others and then make overall conceptualizations about the situations that you encounter. The reason that I bring this up is that when you are depressed, you tend to develop a nasty little schema in which your negative view of yourself leads to a negative interpretation of things that happen to you in the present and eventually to negative predictions about things that have not yet come to pass. You can probably see how having a stable negative schema might lead to the feelings of hopelessness that are common in depression.

One valuable exercise is to try and identify your own schemas. We often apply these as sort of fake rule sets that we hold ourselves to. For instance, we might say something like, "I must get good grades if I want to please my family. They won't love me if I fail. If I don't excel, I have essentially failed." Obviously, these are not completely logical. We don't necessarily say these things verbatim to ourselves, but when you scratch beneath the surface of your assumptions and reactions to everyday situations, sometimes these are what you are left with. Another negative schema might be, "Nobody likes me. People think that I am awkward. I won't ever find love because I am not comfortable around people." Each of these negative patterns serve as one of those shit-colored filters that we talked about and can lead to some pretty serious cognitive errors when we apply them indiscriminately.

I am sure that you are guilty of sometimes overextending these "rules" and applying them to circumstances that they do not fit. For instance, I've had someone tell me about a situation in which their schema about being too awkward to ever find love really bit them in the ass.

34

They were at a get-together at a friend's house (first red flag: if they were *that* awkward, they wouldn't have any friends), and they wound up talking to a girl that they thought was cute and charming. They got on a topic that he was passionate about: video games. Before he knew it, the guard was down and he launched into a mini rant about the state of gaming, microtransactions, and stupid pre-order nonsense. The girl he was talking to said something to the effect of, "Aww how nerdy." Now this simple expression, when filtered through his own unique brand of shit-colored glasses, meant that he was an idiot for revealing his true awkward self and ruining any chance that he might have had. In reality, she was *totally* into it. He learned later on that she actually thought his passionate rant was endearing because it is nice to find a guy who actually gives a shit about anything these days. However, since that possibility did not fit into his narrow negative schema, it didn't even come close to crossing his mind. As a result, *he* started acting like an asshole. He shut down and found a way to abruptly end the conversation. The self-fulfilling prophecy was thus fulfilled.

How do you begin to start recognizing your personal schemas and self-sabotaging thought patterns? Step 1 is to document. I will give you some ideas here, but please don't take these as absolute musts. The key is to do something that works for you and fits with your personality, lifestyle, interests, etc. The point of documenting is to record your thoughts, reactions, and assumptions so that you can start to look at them from a more detached perspective. You might find that the process of tracking and recording these things is like a sort of self-feedback. You don't always realize how you are changing, but simply paying more attention to your patterns and seeing them from a different perspective often leads to improvements. It helps to build your innate sense of what is helpful and what is not, so that you can start to make slight adjustments here and there that combine to make a real difference in your overall mental well-being.

We talked about a great way to identify maladaptive thought patterns in "F**K Anxiety", which is the ABC thought log. I don't want to just repeat myself here, though, so check out the "The Triforce" chapter in that book to learn that technique. A really simple way to get started is making a basic two column chart. One column says "immediate thought" and the other says "reasonable response." This is probably as basic as it gets. Simply write down the immediate thought that you had. In the example that I presented above, it would be something like "She thinks I'm a huge nerd." On the other side, you would put in a more reasonable response. Again, I don't want you to be a rosy optimist. You don't have to be succinct on this side. Brainstorm a bit. You might write "I don't know for certain how she felt. She said 'aww', which usually implies that someone likes something. It actually pisses me off when people pretend like girl gamers don't exist, so maybe she could totally relate. I did not give her the chance to communicate whether she liked what I was saying or whether she was embarrassed to be with me."

Immediate Thought	Reasonable Response
- She thinks I'm lame because I'm a gamer	- Some people LIKE nerds! - Why am I assuming that she isn't a gamer herself? - "Awww" isn't always sarcastic

When you record your thoughts, you usually need to start by logging them at the end of the day or after you are finished with whatever event you have going on. It can be a little difficult to remember everything accurately (especially with your shit-colored glasses), but that is okay. You don't have to get everything "right." Just go over the situations that caused you distress or stuck with you. Write down what you immediately thought or assumed in the situation, and then make yourself a cup of tea and start trying to poke some holes in your brain's asshole logic. The important thing here is to be consistent and do this process as often as you can, especially when you are first getting started. You might even want to do this every night. Eventually, you can begin to log and document during your day on the sly. When you have a lunch break, when you get into your car before driving back home, or even in the moment on a little post it note. The trick is to start migrating your awareness of your cognitive errors and negative schemas closer and closer to the actual event. Over time, you will start to internalize this process and do it in your head automatically, so you don't have to write it down. Then, when you start to achieve a bit of mastery over it, you can apply it in the moment and avoid falling into the same traps that you used to.

The reason I said to do something that works for your particular personality and lifestyle earlier is that there are *many* different creative ways that you can apply these old, fundamental self-help techniques. For some people, having a nice leather bound journal that they can keep next to their bed works best. One creative solution that has worked really well for me is using the voice memo function on my phone. When I am driving on the way back from something and I really need to externalize some of my thoughts, I will pop in my headphones and talk out loud to my phone. To be clear, I only do this when I am driving alone. I'm not *that* weird. There are a couple cool things about logging your thoughts this way. First off, when you have your headphones or ear piece in, It just looks like you are talking on speakerphone, so no one will give you strange glances as they drive by. The other cool thing is that when you get home, you can listen to your own analysis. There is actually some scientific validity to the idea that hearing yourself reason out loud can be very helpful. When you take in information through different mediums, be it written, auditory, or visual, you are giving yourself another avenue to process it. Hearing yourself speak out loud about the ways you are screwing yourself over can allow you to have a more objective perspective and internalize your own voice of reason. Pretty awesome stuff.

There is no limit to the amount of creative ways that you can log your thoughts, reactions, and assumptions. You can blog or vlog about them. You can make visual art. You can write fiction where a person goes through a similar situation, but handles it better. You can create music about them. You can write a rap verse about them. Do something that works for you. If this preference shifts over time that is fine. Just roll with it. What I want you to do is start paying closer attention by recording your thoughts right now, so that you can start reaping the benefits that this perspective provides.

When you have practiced the process of noticing where your assumptions and beliefs go off the rails, you can catch yourself in the moment. Some people can even learn to practice something called cognitive rehearsal. When I was working with people struggling with substance abuse, we would call this "playing the tape through". That means playing the mental video about what might occur and how you might react. This helps you to anticipate roadblocks that may pop up and how you can work to overcome them. You certainly don't have to predict every possible scenario. That is impossible. Instead, you imagine what might happen, notice some of the cognitive mistakes that you have a tendency to make, and craft a few strategies to avoid falling into the same pits of mental douchebaggery that have screwed you over time and time again.

Another effective way to combat these self-sabotaging errors of cognition is to put a name to these thought patterns. (I know I keep saying that I don't want to repeat myself too much on topics that were covered in the previous book, but, damn it some things just deserve restating. Plus I'm probably committing my own cognitive error in assuming that you also have anxiety and decided to read that book as well. I have thrown around a few different terms to describe unhelpful ways of thinking that we sometimes fall into when we are struggling with depression (or a variety of other issues). The classical literature on depression calls these cognitive distortions. They are usually ways of thinking that are not quite reasonable or are overextensions of reasonable thinking. The interesting thing about them is that the ones that rear their ugly heads and lead to depression are actually pretty consistent. Have a look at these and think about whether any of them hit the mark.

Filtering: We pretty much covered this one at the beginning of the chapter. This is where you wear those shit-colored glasses and selectively filter out most of the positive aspects about any given situation.

> *Example:* Say you decided to finally get off your ass and try to take more proactive steps toward fighting against laziness and lethargy by volunteering at a charitable event near you. Objectively, the event was a huge success. The organization made a great deal of money, and the event actually seemed to educate people about a cause that you really care about. However, due to your mental filter, the whole experience felt like a failure to you. You hit traffic on your way there and showed up 15 minutes late. You also feel like you played such a small part that you didn't even need to be there. Seems pretty useless. That is the filtering distortion talking. Taking a step back, there are definitely some alternative points of view that you could try out. Even though being late is not what you intended, shit happens. No one even noticed that you were late, and the event organizers intentionally put in plenty of "buffer" time for people to arrive before the event started. You may feel like you were such a small and insignificant part of this event, but what would happen if every person with a relatively minor part to

play decided to not show up? There would be no event. When you are stuck in filtering mode, it definitely takes some effort to try and see the positive possibilities that you have filtered out.

Overgeneralization: This is one of the more sneaky cognitive distortions, because it does come from a place of logic and reason. However, it takes the lessons that your big human brain has learned from trial and error and overextends them. Our brains are amazing, but they are also kinda lazy. They like to make shortcuts and it is way easier to apply a single rule to everything instead of taking the energy to determine whether a rule applies to each particular circumstance.

Example: A lot of you reading this are probably students. Maybe you have had a teacher or professor that you really did not get along with. For whatever reason you just butted heads and it felt like they were out to get you all year. Believe me, I can relate to this one. During those times of extreme frustration, I took my feelings of anger and sadness and overextended them. I told myself that teachers don't like me. Being an adolescent male, that soon turned into "teachers suck and I don't like them because they don't like me." I'm not a naturally depressive person, so for me this turned into acting out and misbehaving. For someone who does have a tendency toward depression, they might instead turn these feelings inward and take a serious hit to their self-concept. You might wonder what the hell is wrong with you that teachers would hate you so much more than other students. Man, I guess you really just aren't good at school. Of course you don't actually suck at school and not all teachers hate you. In reality, you just have gotten one that you really do not jive well with. Maybe it's something specific about your personal differences, or maybe they are just an asshole. Some teachers are just assholes. Overgeneralization tends to bypass all of this logic, though. It just tells you that you might as well assume that the rule will be true for all similar situations.

Personalization: This is a tricky one that often leads to those nasty feelings of guilt. Basically you hold yourself personally accountable for things that you may not have even played a part in. You have gotten so used to things being your fault, it's almost like your default mode now.

> *Example:* For those parents out there, you may have had a situation where your child is acting or performing poorly in school. This is a very easy one to personalize, especially if you have a depressive streak. The depressed brain is going to immediately jump to self-blame, and you will start taking guesses at what you did or didn't do that might have influenced your kiddo's behavior. In reality, there are a lot of factors that could be at play. Maybe there is something social going on like bullying or even something positive like a new romantic interest that has made your child's attention much more divided. It is completely possible that you have had some influence on the situation, but it isn't reasonable to automatically assume that the whole deal is your fault.

Fallacy of Control: The fallacy of control takes both external and internal forms. For external, you feel that there are many things that are outside of your control that affect your life and emotional state. Things keep happening to you and it's so annoying that you can't do anything about it! The fallacy of internal control is very much like the personalization that we talked about above. You assume that you somehow have control over the way other people act or feel.

> *Example:* Your boss at work is a jerk. He keeps pushing you harder and harder to make ridiculous deadlines and

changing the things that you are responsible for. On top of that, you can't catch a break with traffic. And now it's raining. UGH why does this stuff keep happening to me? Why won't the universe just let me be happy (external)? Oh, and now the boss is being an asshole again. Wonder what I did this time (internal)?

Emotional Reasoning: In this one, things get a little twisted. It's probably one of the most common distortions of thinking that happens with or without depression. Instead of having a situation lead to you feeling a certain way, the emotion comes first and colors your perception of what is going on. Basically you assume that since you feel a certain way, it must be true, regardless of what the objective evidence says.

> *Example:* You don't know exactly why, but you wake up feeling like nobody is on your side and you are fighting an uphill battle to please anyone. This causes you to be pretty jumpy and on guard throughout the day. You start to see everything that your friends and family do as an expression of them being tired of you and eventually convince yourself that it's true. So, naturally, they start to notice that something is a bit off and ask you what's wrong. Since you assume that your internal feelings are correct and that they don't actually care, you just respond with a brusque and unconvincing "I'm fine." This naturally leads them to assume that you just want to be left alone, and then when they give you space, you take it as more evidence that they were sick of you in the first place. Another vicious cycle.

Labeling: You apply a global label to things instead of thinking about them on a case by case basis. Instead of saying that you fucked up a particular situation this one time, you label yourself as a fuck up and take on the emotional hit to the groin that comes along with that label.

Example: You're a student and you have just bombed a test. I don't mean that you made a few little mistakes here and there, I'm talking a defcon 1 level total botch. Enough that your teacher actually asked you to talk to them after class because it seemed unusual. Well, instead of taking stock of the situation and noticing that you probably did poorly this one time because you were sick and couldn't sleep the night before, you label yourself a bad student. Only bad students have to talk to the teacher right?

So, the thing about cognitive distortions is that we all do them sometimes. You're a damn liar if you say otherwise. It's not rocket science to see how these can make you feel pretty shitty. I bet some of you read through those and went, "Yep. Oh yeah, that's me. Damn... that's me too. Okay, this is just getting ridiculous now." Don't you fret. My aim is not only to point out the ways in which your brain is a douche, but also give you some strategies to overcome its douchiness. The first step is arming yourself with the knowledge of which are your personal roadblocks. My list here is certainly not an exhaustive one. I just wanted to provide you a few examples that probably apply to a good number of you. If you are interested in looking at a more extensive list of them, a simple Google search of "cognitive distortions" should do the trick.

A mentor of mine does some awesome sports psychology work. With his competitive cyclists, he describes an exercise called "mapping your monsters." Basically, this acknowledges that they already know the course for the race they're about to ride. They know the hills, they know the turns, and they know which portions of the race are going to give them hell, based on their past experience riding. When you map your monsters, you draw out the course and literally mark where each monster is probably going to reside. For one reason or another, simply noticing what the problems are and where they arise helps to take away some of their power to screw you over. I think bringing your own cognitive monsters out into the light also takes away some of their power. So you can start by using my list here (or any list that you find online) and highlighting the ones that most apply to you. Then you can make a little log like this:

	M	T	W	Th	F
Filtering	|||	||	₩	||	
Personalization	||||	₩			||||	
Overgeneralization	||	|||	||	₩	

Start off by logging each time you engage in these unhelpful thinking patterns each day. You can quickly get an idea about where you're shooting yourself in the foot. It's alright if this is a bit shocking to you. That's part of the process. By writing it down in a log like this, you are again externalizing the information. You are allowing yourself to look at it from a more detached and objective perspective. This sort of feedback is already your first step toward decreasing the frequency with which you run into these mental traps. To be clear, the point here is not self-flagellation. I don't want you to punish yourself each time you engage in a cognitive distortion. Instead, keep striving to engage in them less and use this valuable insider information to guide you on your quest.

All or nothing thinking is a pretty big problem in depression. You tell yourself that something was a failure if it did not go completely right, and that makes you feel really terrible. Remember how I said that I want you to be a realist instead of a rosy optimist? You can acknowledge that you have fucked up without engaging in all-or-nothing thinking. Instead of just writing the entire situation off as a fail, try rating it on a scale from 0-100. I know this might seem a little pessimistic, and many other self-help resources might tell you to avoid telling yourself that you screwed up at all. To me, that approach is really unfair. We are human and all screw up sometimes. We want to get better at realistically judging just to what extent we have screwed up and to get better at emotionally reacting in a way that is consistent with that rating instead of always reacting in an over-the-top dramatic fashion. I tend to use being late to work or class as an example of a basic mistake because it's unfortunately an inherited disposition that my family handed down to me, and I have had to learn to not let it wreck my mood for the entire day.

Sure, being late and causing some sort of disruption is upsetting. It is probably your own damn fault, and you should feel bad about it. How bad, though? This is where that 0-100 scale comes in. Does anything about your lateness indicate that you won't be able to do good things with the rest of your day? Have you been late before and been able to salvage your day just fine? The other day, I was late to a treatment team meeting. I blamed traffic (external control fallacy) when it was probably my fault, and I did cause a bit of disruption. The members of the team were gracious and didn't make any comments while they shifted around to make room for me. In that moment, my brain was trying to convince me that I screwed up the meeting and probably my whole day. Taking a step back, I used this 0-100 scale based on how smooth the rest of the meeting went and my ability to contribute useful information. Absolutely it was my fault and I felt like an idiot, but I really only hit a 20 on the fuck up scale. In my own silly brain, that allowed me to only feel 20% like shit. That's the trick. I don't want you to think magical pixie dust thoughts and hope that you can do whatever you want without consequence just because you think positively. You still need to handle your stuff. However, you can be more realistic and try to work toward having emotional reactions that are appropriate to the situation instead of using that deadly combination of emotional reasoning and all-or-nothing thinking to drive you straight into Depressionville every time you might the slightest mistake.

Using the "fuck up scale" instead of defaulting to all-or-nothing thinking patterns takes some practice. Your depressed brain is in the habit of blowing things out of proportion, so when you first start trying out this technique, your ratings might be inflated. That's another place where those people who you recruited as your logical barometers can come in handy. You can explain the circumstances and ask them how they would rate it on the 0-100 scale. Then, you can compare your rating to theirs. After a while, you will get the hang of more realistically appraising your own fuck ups, so just stick with it.

Another valuable tool that you can use to fight back against your brain's lazy shortcuts is related to that labelling distortion we talked about before. That is the one where you apply mean labels to yourself instead of just describing what you did or didn't do in that particular instance. The trick that you can use here is also one that we use in the world of science. You can define your terms. When you are doing a science experiment and you want to look at a given construct like happiness, relationship strength, or effectiveness of a drug, you need to come up with something called an *operational definition*. This means that you need to find a very specific way to describe and define that construct so that we know exactly how it is measured and someone else across the globe can also investigate the same thing.

In the same way, you can push yourself to specifically define the labels that you find yourself using. When you call yourself a failure, an idiot, a bad spouse, a bad child, or a loner, what exactly do you mean by that? What are the specific traits that an idiot possesses? What sorts of actions do they take? Who can you think of that certainly exemplifies those specific traits? Are you just the same as them? In what ways are you different from that person? I know those were a lot of questions in a row, but ideally that's what your pattern of thinking should start to look like. Use some Socratic questioning to poke holes in your distorted thinking and your global labelling. It's alright if there are some aspects about you as a person or about what you have done that fit with the specific label that you have defined. You can do idiotic things sometimes without being an idiot.

Here's another personal example: I consider myself to be a pretty nice person overall. I care about humans and don't ever mean to intentionally put someone down. My own personal golden rule is "just don't be an asshole". Well, that works out well most of the time for me, but believe it or not, I'm not perfect (GASP!) and sometimes I slip up and say something that I instantly regret. I don't remember the exact conversation, but I was chatting with my wife over dinner and said something that I thought was very casual and playful, but to her it was a pretty sharp attack on her character. At first, I had no idea why I started getting the silent treatment. Once I probed a bit, I saw how what I said could definitely be taken as criticism. Even though I apologized, it was clear that the damage was done and there was no taking it back. Now, I don't want you to think that this was some catastrophic event in my marriage. It wasn't. Just one of the normal misunderstandings that happen among spouses. However, I really needed to catch myself in that moment. What I said is certainly something that an asshole might say, but that does not mean that I am an asshole.

If I were a depressed person, I would not be so easily convinced that I was not an asshole. I would have to get specific about what exactly qualifies someone as an asshole. Well, I can think of a few people that I will not name that fit the bill. They tend to have traits like not caring about anyone else and seeming to enjoy making other people upset. Do these apply to me? Hell no. I HATE making other people upset over something that I did… probably to a fault. I can't let it go until I feel like I've fixed it. In this previous example, I may have communicated through my actions that I don't care, but the fact that it is eating me up so much inside indicates that I actually do. I am still allowed to feel a bit shitty about it. I messed up, but going through this sort of self-analysis and being more specific and investigative about labels helps that be a temporary feeling of ickiness that goes away instead of serving as just another log on the depressive fire.

The other thing to consider, when it comes to labels, is that they always have a flip-side. Sometimes, it can be useful to examine the other side of the coin. Even though the immediate label that you give yourself such as "greedy", "asshole", "idiot", or "failure" may have a clear negative weight to them, you can also ask yourself whether there are some positive qualities in there as well. For example, if you are dealing with the asshole label, you might be able to look at the other side of the coin by breaking it down a little more. What are some positive aspects of assholeness? Maybe you are a skeptical person. That's definitely an admirable quality which can enable you to think critically and get to the heart of important issues. Maybe you are assertive. That's also great in a lot of ways. Many people never learn how to stand up for themselves and instead get stepped on by other people every day. With this example, you are not throwing out the label entirely, you are just recognizing that there are some nuances to it. You can own both the good and the bad. You can notice that you screwed up overall, but, in some ways, it was just a case of admirable qualities getting out of hand. That is much easier to learn from. You can adjust your behavior with information like that.

I've made a lot of references to scientists in this chapter. I really want you to internalize that idea. Create a mental picture of yourself in a silly white lab coat with protective glasses or whatever image really screams scientist to you. Adopt this little mental alter ego when you find yourself engaging in these unhelpful patterns of thinking. You don't have to walk around all day, analyzing and questioning everything (unless that's already your personality), but you can switch into this mode when you need to examine the evidence that your silly brain tries to immediately pass off as fact. Of course, any good scientist knows the importance of documenting your findings. That's why your grade school science teachers made you write down every detail in those little composition books during lab. It is exceptionally hard to see yourself changing on a day to day basis. If you've ever trained physically for something, you know that this is true. If you are trying to gain muscle definition, lose weight, or complete your race faster, you really can't see much difference from one day to the next. However, when you keep track of your progress through pictures, or logging your performance in a paper or digital log, it becomes much easier to see change across weeks or months. Fighting back against depression can be much the same way. Remember; your brain is currently trained to tell you, "See? That did nothing. The same shit happened again, just like always. This book is useless and you are not getting any better." When that happens, you can whip out your log and determine whether that is true or not. You can say, "Well let's slow down here. Sure I made the same mistake that I did yesterday, but it looks like overall the number of times that I am engaging in distorted thinking has gone down by 20% over the past month. That's the difference between a D and an F in just 30 days. Pretty badass if you ask me!"

It's also important to admit that sometimes the things we try are not hitting the mark and making a big difference for us. There is nothing wrong with that. Part of being a good scientist is being open to the null hypothesis that no change has occurred after trying something new. Learning that a particular strategy just isn't your thing is also really valuable information. By continuously documenting and logging your progress, you can notice when things aren't quite working for you and make the choice to change course. Maybe it's a slight adjustment to the strategies that you are using, or maybe you need to do a radical overhaul of your approach. No matter what, you will never know that it is time to shift your approach if you don't take the time to analyze your own progress and check in with yourself. Documenting makes it that much easier to take an objective look at your progress and make those decisions. Eventually, you will become amazing at fine tuning and tweaking your approach to really work for you.

Ch. 4 A Chapter About Suicide

Time to be straight up. I want to talk about suicide. That's right, I said it. Suicide. Some people seem to think that suicide is like Voldemort and we should never utter the name out loud, or that it's like Beetlejuice and if we say it three times, suddenly someone will decide to kill themselves. That's not how it works. In fact, I think that a lot of people kill themselves because it *isn't* talked about. In this chapter I'm going to talk about it. I would say "trigger warning," but I wouldn't mean it. It's something that we need to talk about and something that we need to stand up to.

Suicidality is a spectrum. Most of us have had the passing thought about what things would be like if we were gone or what it would feel like to die. Probably fewer of us have made a game plan and identified the method and circumstances that we would use to kill ourselves if we felt the need to. I think that we all lie somewhere on this continuum. Yes, being on the extreme end of it is dangerous, but just because you may fall farther to one side of this spectrum than the other does not mean that you are crazy or that you are hopeless.

We have to get into a few terms here because I think that they get thrown around pretty casually, and I want to make sure that you understand them. The first one that I want to clarify is "suicidal ideation." The term sounds scary and intimidating, but it's not too bad. Suicidal ideation just means that you are thinking of suicide. On the lower end of this spectrum, it crosses your mind every once in a while and on the high end of spectrum, you are virtually obsessed with the idea of killing yourself. A word with a very different tone is "suicidal intent." The word intent is a little scarier because it refers to the degree to which you plan to kill yourself at some point. Finally, it is important to understand the term means. This references the method that you might use to kill yourself (gun, bridge, knife etc.). Let me use a hypothetical example here to illustrate how these terms are used in a practical way.

So, let's say that we are trying to understand Sally, who is a 23 year old recent college graduate who just suffered the loss of her mother and has been unemployed for the past 6 months like many others in her cohort. She certainly has a lot going on, but where does she fit on the suicidality spectrum? Sally has had fleeting thoughts about death during the rough patches throughout her life, but she currently can't seem to get the thought of it out of her head. No matter how hard she tries to shake them off, thoughts of death seem to creep into every empty space in her brain. Her little internal voice tells her that this is all just too much to deal with. She envisions herself taking every medication in her bathroom cabinet and falling asleep in a hot bath. This scares the shit out of her. She really does not want to die. In fact, she feels like she *has* to live for the rest of her family ... it's just so damn scary having these thoughts. For now, she feels very confident that she will not try to kill herself and she wants it to stay that way.

Okay, sorry if that was a little intense. I just wanted to give you a realistic scenario to wrap your head around. In this case, Sally definitely has suicidal ideation that is at least moderate if not severe. She is really preoccupied with the thought of dying. However, her fear of death and desire to find a way to live indicates that her intent is actually pretty low. Even though her intent is low at the moment, her level of ideation is definitely worthy of concern. For that reason, we want to be careful about her means of killing herself. She identified one for us, which was taking the pills in her cabinet. In this scenario, it might be a good idea to enlist some help to make sure that she is able to maintain her safety as well as she wants to.

I'm going to ask you to do something pretty damn brave for me here. You can do it. I want you to compare yourself to

Sally. Right now, in this moment, where do you lie in the dimensions of suicidal ideation, intent, and means? There is no wrong answer here, but it is important for you to know. If your intent is high and you have a means that comes to mind immediately, I want you to seriously consider putting this book down right now and getting help. If you are in the United States, you can call 1-800-273-8255. This is the national suicide prevention hotline where people are trained to help you stay safe. If you live in another country, you can google "suicide hotline" and find some options near you. Depending on the country, you might need to adjust the words slightly. For instance, in some countries the translation for "suicide" is closer to "self-murder", so play around with the terminology until you find what you are looking for. If you don't want to deal with a hotline and would rather just get the hell out of dodge, you can call 911 or your country's equivalent emergency services number. If you tell them that you are worried about killing yourself, they will come out and do an assessment with you and, if necessary, take you to a hospital where you will be kept safe. I know this doesn't sound fun (and it probably isn't), but this is not the time to think about convenience. We are talking about the permanent destruction of your life here. As far as I'm concerned, that's the most pure example of a medical emergency there is.

I want you to live. Suicidality that comes from depression is often a symptom that stems from the hopelessness that we talked about earlier. Your asshole of a brain in tricking you into thinking that there is no way out of your situation and no point in hoping for anything different in the future. The old saying still definitely rings true: suicide is a permanent solution to a temporary situation. Don't make that mistake, my friend. Things *can* change, even if your douchebrain won't let you believe that right now.

If you aren't quite on the crisis/emergency side of the suicidality spectrum, there are some other things that you can do to help yourself cope. My first advice would be not keeping it a secret. I know that talking about suicide is scary as hell, and it should be. It's a frightening prospect. However, keeping it a secret only gives it more power. Take the power back, my friend. Drawing suicidality out into the open can be one of the most protective things that you can do. I don't mean getting on Facebook and shouting it from the rooftops (unless that is really your style). I mean that you should tell your family, your significant other, your closest friends, or your doctor.

One of the terrifying things about bringing up the topic of suicide is the prospect of people overreacting. I think some people imagine that as soon as they utter the word suicide, a Special Forces group will breach their wall or rappel down from helicopters and violently extract them straight to a mental hospital. That's not going to happen. Your family might react strongly for sure, but that's because you are important to them. It may also be a big shock to them to hear this from you, because you are better at hiding these thoughts than you realize. Of course this is personally loaded. We don't all have good families, but I hope you see the point that I'm trying to make. If the people that you tell about your suicidal thoughts overreact, educate them about where you lie on those spectrums we talked about, and help them understand what your level of intent is at the moment. If you aren't looking to kill yourself in the immediate future, let them know, and also tell them that it *is* something that you are struggling with. Tell them that you need them to be on your team while you find your way out of these scary and confusing feelings. I know that it can be very difficult to find the right words to say in situations like this. Just try your best. The words don't need to come out right. They just need to come out.

So, you tell people that you have been thinking about killing yourself. Groovy. What now? Well, there are a few things that they can do to help. All of this comes down to the level of severity that you are experiencing with your suicidality. (It is a little bit difficult to write in generalities, so please pardon anything that doesn't directly apply to you here.) One thing that most families or friends would be happy to do is limit your access to the likely means of killing yourself. The scenario that I described with Sally earlier is actually quite common. Pills are an easily accessible, non-violent means of ending a life. If you are on a prescription medication or have access to drugs that have overdose potential, such as Xanax or strong pain killers, consider buying a tiny safe for the storage of those pills and giving the key to someone that you trust. You can keep a small amount for treatment or emergency, but not enough on hand that you could possibly hurt yourself. If you need to access the whole bottle for any reason, you must go through that trusted person. The point of this strategy isn't just to take away your autonomy. In fact, if you live alone and have no access to trusted people to help out, I would still encourage you to try out the safe method. The trick here is giving yourself intermediate steps. When you are in crisis, your brain tries to trick you into jumping from point A to point Z. Crisis states are temporary. If you include things designed to put more time between the impulse to kill yourself and your means of doing it, you will give yourself more opportunities to make a different, non-fatal choice.

You know how fire extinguishers usually have that bold text on their storage cases that says **IN CASE OF EMERGENCY BREAK GLASS**? In this method, you make your own "in case of emergency" box. With my patients, I have often made this literal by using a display case with glass on the front. (If your means of suicide includes cutting yourself, please use your noggin and don't include the actual breaking of glass in your method. Just make a box with a latch or something.) Anyways, the box itself is something that you fill up when you are feeling your best, most hopeful self. When you have some clarity about your desire to live. Fill it with pictures of people you care about, movie releases that you are looking forward to, clippings of grass, a Rubik's Cube, a list of 20 reasons to stay alive...

whatever makes sense to you as a person. Think of this as the emotional version of the shot of adrenaline that action heroes stab themselves with in the movies when things are most dire, and they need to somehow get their broken body to push through another hour of over-the-top destruction. It is a quick shot of hope, reality, and reasonable thinking designed to postpone you taking action during the peak of your crisis, allowing you to reach out for emergency help if needed.

Talking to your friends or family about your suicidal thoughts is one thing, but telling a professional like your doctor or therapist is much more risky, right? Well, I wouldn't call it risky. It is certainly a different experience, because most medical professionals as well as people in helping roles like psychologists, therapists, and social workers are mandated by law to report you if they are concerned that you might be a danger to yourself. However, this isn't just an off-the-cuff judgment. The professional needs to evaluate you to see what your level of risk is. If you are just having thoughts, but have no intent and no immediate means, you probably wouldn't expect any immediate action. However, after careful evaluation, if your doctor suspects that you are in serious risk of harming yourself, you can be held for your own safety. I know this sounds harsh, but I want to stress to you that this DOES NOT happen every time you talk about these topics.

Let me put it into perspective for you. Over the past year, I was working in a major healthcare setting, seeing probably around 15 new patients every week. I talked about suicide with probably 100 of them, and there was only one case that I ended up collaborating with to work out a voluntary hospitalization.

Just like I suggested with your loved ones, be honest and clear with any professionals that you tell about these issues. Help them understand that you need support and how confident you may or may not feel about your personal safety in the moment. It is SO important to keep your providers aware of your situation in terms of suicidality. In some cases, it could even be related to a medication side effect. In others, they will simply want to be checking in with you over time to make sure that things haven't taken a downward turn.

When your doctor or helping professional evaluates you, there are a few things that they will be looking for. In addition to assessing you ideation, intent, and means, they will want to know if you have had any previous suicide attempts. Previous attempts are actually the largest predictor of future attempts, so that is something that would definitely to communicate to them. They also want to see what you are living for. I always ask, "On a scale of 0 to 10, where 10 is completely confident in your safety and 0 is the opposite, how do you feel today?" When the patient answers, I follow up with, "Why not lower?" Even if they are at a pretty low 3 out of 10 on this scale, their answer will tell me some valuable information about what is still keeping them alive at this moment. Clinicians will also want to look at things like your level of guilt, any substances that you might be taking, and what type of social supports that you have. Trust me, any doctor would be *much* happier to enlist the help of you family and send you home into their loving arms to keep you safe than send you to a hospital, if that is a reasonable option.

Let's say that your doctor does determine that you are at serious risk of harming yourself and would like to put you on a hold to ensure your safety. What does that look like? This is another area that is hard to write about in generalities. I'll tell you about what it looks like in good ol' California, USA, where I practice. In my state, if a doctor, peace officer, or other qualified clinician determines, after their careful assessment, that you are at immediate risk of harming yourself, they may place you under an "involuntary hold" for a few days. This is a way to keep you safe in the short term and hopefully connect you to resources that will allow you to move forward with your life with support while lowering the risk of harming yourself. Let me be the first to say that I 100% understand that this possibility sounds terrifying. I know it does. However, it's really super-important to know that being hospitalized for suicidality does not mean you are going to live out One Flew Over the Cuckoo's Nest or wind up in Arkham Asylum. Let me paint a more realistic picture.

When you hear the term "hospitalization", it makes you think of sanitariums and other scary clinical settings. While there is definitely some variability in quality between the different psych hospitals out there, in general they are designed to be as comfortable as possible. They will look much like any other clinic or hospital you've visited. When you arrive to the hospital, you will undergo an intake process in which your belongings will be collected and documented. You are usually allowed to have some personal items with you. However, they may temporarily confiscate any items that could be used in a suicide attempt. For example, you probably won't be keeping glass items or clothes with drawstrings because an actively suicidal person could use those to harm themselves. You will most likely also undergo a short psychiatric evaluation. In many cases, they already have some information from the person or agency that referred you, but they will want to make sure that they get a good picture of your current state, medically and psychologically. After going through your intake, you will be given a room. This is where you will be sleeping while you are staying at the hospital, and frequently you will be cohabitating with a roommate. It's no Holiday Inn, but it's not a jail cell either.

At the hospital, you will meet a large range of people. There will be those who probably would not have actually killed themselves, but are just not completely confident in their own safety. There will also be those who are talking to themselves, yelling in the night, and convinced that the staff is trying to poison them. This can be jarring, but it can also give you some much needed perspective on your own situation. You will have a few different evaluations with therapists and doctors during your stay. Their goal is to help stabilize you, develop a plan for moving forward, and to get you back out into the world. You will also be expected to attend groups intended to help you build coping skills and learn ways to regulate your emotions. It can be a bit overwhelming and scary for sure. Luckily, you are usually able to speak on the phone at certain times of the day and may have loved ones come to visit you. Sleeping is usually a bit restless in the hospital because it's unfamiliar, and you are checked on throughout the night to ensure that you are still safe. It's annoying, but it's necessary. You will be discharged from the hospital when your hold has expired and when the doctors feel confident in your personal safety. You won't just be dumped out on the curb with no plan. The whole idea is to help ride out your crisis, give you some skills to take with you out the door, and to develop a follow up plan with mental health providers in the community to keep you going in a positive direction once you are back out in the world.

I won't lie to you. Being hospitalized is tough. It isn't a fun experience. However, sometimes it is absolutely the right choice. Looking back on her hospitalization, someone that I know in my personal life made a metaphor that has always stuck with me. She said that she hated going to the hospital. She felt guilty that she had to go, and she just wanted to come home once she got there. However, she said that she would never take back the experience, because it was a necessary step in her recovery. She described it like a broken bone. Sometimes when you break a bone, the doctors will have to re-break it in order to set the bone in the proper position for healing. Being hospitalized for your safety serves the purpose of resetting you and putting you on the path toward healing. I hope it is something that you do not need to deal with. However, I hope you now have a better picture of what the process looks like if it does come to that. It's nothing to be ashamed of. Sometimes it is just one important step on the path to overcoming depression.

The final topic I want to address in this chapter is self-harm without suicidal intent. In the field we call it non-suicidal self-injury (NSSI). NSSI is an interesting topic because it can serve several purposes. I think the most common reaction to NSSI (by people who have never been through it) is to interpret it, especially the cutting variety, as a "cry for help." While that can certainly be the case, there is often much more to it. If you cut, scratch, slam, burn, rip, or engage in any other variety of self-harm, you know what I'm talking about. Many times it is *used* as a tool. Self-harm is often a coping skill. It's not a good one, and it's not safe, but it is a coping skill. Sometimes it occurs when things are too overwhelming and you want to feel like you at least have control over your own body. Other times, it happens when you are so numb and anhedonic that it seems like the only way you can actually feel something. I want you to think of NSSI as a symptom. That tells you that you need a coping skill that you haven't been able to locate yet, and this is what you are using in the meantime. If you are in the NSSI camp, I do not want you to be ashamed, but I do want you to try to stop. A solid portion of completed suicides are accidental, and I do not want you to die. As you may have noticed, there is also often a diminishing return effect that happens with self-injury. It's almost like an addiction where you need more and more physical feedback to have any emotional effect. That is a slippery slope.

If you engage in NSSI, the best course would be to get professional help. It is something that you can transition out of as you find more healthy ways of coping. Many people are scared about the prospect of bringing their self-injury up to their parents or to their doctors. I know it's scary, but I will echo my sentiment at the beginning of this chapter by saying: your permanent health needs to outweigh your temporary discomfort or embarrassment at this time. Another worry is how your doctors will react when you tell them. I want to stress to you that they should not simply sweep you away to a hospital if you tell them that you cut yourself. If you want to be very sure that they understand, you will need to tell them *why* you cut. Tell them the purpose that it has served, that you don't want to die, and why you need help stopping.

In the meantime, I would like to give you one tip that could possibly help you scale back on your self-injurious behavior until you can get in to see a professional. I absolutely need to mention that this particular approach has not been researched for NSSI in particular, but I think that it could potentially apply. There has been some research indicating that puzzle games such as Bejeweled, Tetris, or Candy Crush can help to reduce the strength of cravings. The reason this research may be relevant here is that NSSI is sometimes very much like an addiction. From what I have learned from people who self-harm, they are often fighting a losing battle with the growing thought of it. Even if they don't want to do it, they can visualize themselves cutting, burning, or whatever method, and the more they try to push the thought away, the bigger and more vivid it gets. With these puzzle games, they basically override the portion of your brain responsible for temporarily storing visual information. It doesn't mean that you won't be able to visualize yourself going through with the self-injury, but now it will be competing for mental real estate with the puzzle you are working on. I'll stress again that this is an extrapolation on the existing research and this particular method has not been supported yet, **but** it is essentially a zero risk strategy to try out for yourself. So, next time you find yourself starting to picture the process or the release of your self-injurious method, instead reach for your phone and play 10 minutes of a puzzle game. See if that brings down your urge enough to make a more healthy decision. I'm sure I don't need to say it, but this is not a substitute for professional help. You still need to do that. This is just an in the moment coping strategy that you can try out.

Phew! We made it, guys. I know that was a tough chapter. It can be hard to hear these things. I'm proud of you for making it through. If this chapter really struck a nerve with you and you feel like there are some immediate steps that you need to take in order to invest in your own safety, please go do those right now. I will be here when you get back.

Ch. 5 On letting Go

One of the biggest roadblocks that has been shared with me by people actively contending with depression is the tendency to dwell on the shit that has already gone wrong. I totally get it. All of the strategies and tidbits of enlightened information are great, but what good are they if you don't even have the mental real estate to put them into practice? You can't begin your journey of a single step if you are too crushed by your feelings to get up off of the floor. All too often, guilt, frustration, and anger from the past keep you held back. Allow me to tell you the story of the annoying party guest.

So let's say that you are having a party. Not a giant rager, but a sizeable get together with friends and family. Everyone arrives at your place, and you find yourself hopping around from group to group saying hello and joining in on the different conversations taking place. It's a wonderful day and you are really enjoying yourself. That Is until **they** show up. We all have one... the annoying co-worker or classmate that thinks they are your friend, but they most certainly are **not**. You didn't invite them to this get together, but alas... here they are. Ugh! They are so annoying. What are they doing here? You don't even like them! So you go over to them, try to politely express that you were not expecting them over, and drop some pretty non-subtle hints that they should probably leave.

Alright. Problem solved. You think you made yourself pretty clear and got rid of the unfortunate character. You go back to the party and get caught up in a new conversation about the latest blockbuster movies or something like that. Then, you hear it. That annoying-ass voice from the other room. They are STILL HERE. WTF?! You tell your friends that you will be right back and excuse yourself to the other room. This time you are a little more forceful and tell them flat out that they are not welcome in your home. You tell them that they need to leave.

Good job! Peace is restored. A few minutes pass, and you think that your efforts were successful. Your moment of glory is fleeting, though. Before you know it, that persistent douchecanoe (technical term) is back again, trying to buddy up with the other guests. They are totally killing the vibe. This time you've had enough. You lose your filter of politeness and tell them to get the hell out of your house before there is serious trouble.

This relentless pattern is maddening and exhausting. You just want to enjoy your freaking party, but here you are managing this idiot's behavior, and before you realize it... people start heading home. You just missed your own party, and that royally sucks. The worst part is that this isn't the first time something like this has happened. Cue frustration, guilt, anger, and all of those other fun things. I'm sure you can see the parallels here between the party scenario and the battle going on with the thoughts in your own head. Whether it be a nagging self-doubt, a sense of guilt about something, lingering anger about some injustice, or an obsessive worry about something that hasn't even happened yet, sometimes these thoughts seem to exhaust all of your mental horsepower. The more you fight back, the bigger they grow and the more disruptive they become, just like that annoying party guest.

Here's another approach. Let's go back to the party scenario. Imagine that when that obnoxious dummy came by in the first place, you didn't fight back so hard. They may not be your friend, but they aren't exactly your arch nemesis either. Sometimes, you can just let them be that annoying party guest. Sure, you still notice that they are there, but once you decide to let them do their own thing, it seems like they don't quite have as much power over you. You aren't constantly leaving your own fun moments to deal with them. It can even be amusing in a television sitcom sort of way. Oh, there's the annoying party guest again! Look at them being lame and bugging the crap out of my uncle in the other room [Cue studio laugh track]. This does not mean that you've lost the battle. Let me say that again. This does **not** mean that you have lost the battle. It just means that you are not playing their game this time. You can have great conversations and thoroughly enjoy your party in the presence of this annoying party guest.

I hope you can see the parallel to your own thinking patterns here as well. Just like the annoying party guest, you are not pretending that those thoughts and feelings do not exist. You are simply deciding to not let them run the show. You are acknowledging that they are there and then bringing your attention back to your ongoing party. In a certain way, that acknowledgment that they do exist helps to take away some of their ability to derail you. This shift of perspective that I have been describing is typically referred to as mindfulness- a term that has been a huge buzzword in the field of mental health for some time now. The reason it has become such a popular concept is that it seems to suggest a very different approach from the more cognitive based approaches, which try to help you actively fight back against your thoughts. In my opinion cognitive approaches and mindfulness actually play really well together. I think that you 100% need to fight back against the depressive mindset, but you also need to get better at sitting with the thoughts and feelings that you do have and recognize that they are not always so threatening. Let me explain mindfulness in another way.

So clouds, right? They are awesome. You can lay on your back and look up at them and see all kinds of things. Some of them are big and fluffy, like they would make an awesome bed to go take a nap on. Some of them are kinda gross and unhealthy looking. Maybe some of them remind of you different animals (I always seem to see dragons). Obviously, each of these different interpretations (comfy bed, gross darkness, awesome dragon) brings about different feelings as they pass into your awareness. Here's the thing, though. They are all made of the same stuff. They are just water vapor up in the air. That's it. And if we keep lying there and looking up, we can notice that the clouds will drift into our awareness, and if we allow ourselves to not fixate on them, they gently float past as well. I think of our thoughts as being just like these clouds. Some of them are happy thoughts, some of them are worrisome, perhaps some are even a bit scary. They are just thoughts though. We may have our own different interpretations of them and we like to apply labels like "good" and "bad" to them, but in the end they are just thoughts.

Often, we get stuck on thoughts and get into these huge, annoying battles with them. If instead, we take a moment to acknowledge them, just like those clouds up in the sky, they will continue to drift through our awareness at the same pace as any other thought we might have. As humans, we have a tendency to engage in something called "fusion", where we fuse our thoughts and our behaviors together. We saw a bit of this in the motivation chapter. I feel like a bum, therefore I can't get anything done today. In reality, you can feel any sort of way and also act in whatever way you would like. It's not being ungenuine or lying to yourself. It's about allowing your thoughts, emotions, and other private internal experiences to exist and not necessarily dictate all of the actions that you take. The mindful approach really helps us to move forward in our quest to eliminate depression, or rather to reduce the impact that we allow depression to have on us.

The thing about mindfulness is that it definitely takes some practice. It's not a difficult concept to understand, but sometimes putting it into practice is a different story. Don't worry. I got you covered. I have a simple exercise that you can do to start training yourself to be more mindful and less judgmental about your own thoughts and internal experiences. When I say training, I mean it. Think of this as a skill that you can get better and better at. So, the exercise itself is a simple breathing exercise. It is a bit different than some of the breathing exercises you have probably encountered before.

Many of those are designed to put you into a state of relaxation or to relieve stress. It's possible that this exercise could have that effect on you, but that's not really the point. Okay. Okay. Let me just explain the damn thing.

You already have a head start in this mindful breathing exercise, because step 1 is to breathe. That's it. Just breathe. If step 1 is a problem for you... you might want to make sure that you aren't actually a ghost. The cool thing about this is you don't have to do any particular sort of breathing. You don't need to change anything. I just want you to draw your attention to your breathing. Notice your breath. Pick a place in your body that you can really feel that breath. This can be different each time. Just notice where you can feel it in your body in this moment. Maybe it is the rise and fall of your belly. Maybe it is the expanding and contracting of your chest. Maybe it is the cool air rushing into your nose and the warm air flowing out of your mouth. Like I said, just notice the place that your breath is apparent to you right now.

Now, being human (presumably), in a few seconds your mind is going to start to wander. You will realize that you are no longer focusing on the physical sensations of your breath, and instead you are thinking about what you are going to do in an hour, trying to remember if you forgot something important, feeling emo over a recent break up, or getting angry because that damn commercial jingle is still stuck in your head after 4 days straight. That's great! You are supposed to get distracted. That's where the training part comes in.

When the spotlight of your attention leaves your breath and instead shines on some other thought or feeling, I don't want you to try to force it out of your head. Instead, allow it to sit in the spotlight for a moment, and give it a few seconds of acknowledgment. Allow yourself to identify what the thought or feeling is. Once you've given it a moment in the spotlight, gently redirect that spotlight of attention back to your breath. And that's it! It's seriously so simple. Don't get frustrated when you find yourself moving your attention away from your breath very frequently at first. Be excited about it. Every time you get distracted by some thought or feeling, it is another chance to practice this attentional shift.

I seriously love this exercise. It's beautifully simple. At first it is SO hard, though. Your distractions per minute will be too damn high. Keep practicing it! I know it might be hard to understand the usefulness of paying A LOT of attention to your breathing. The secret is, it's not about breathing at all. It's about becoming better and better at noticing your thoughts and feelings and not letting them derail you. It's about growing in your ability to intentionally shift your attention back to the thing that you are focusing on. If we are continuing the spotlight metaphor, imagine that you are making a transition from a newbie spotlight operator to a seasoned theater veteran who can shift that light to any subject at a moment's notice. You don't necessarily need to have intruding thoughts or feelings any less. You can just become better and more efficient at quickly shaking hands with your distractions and then redirecting your attention back to the matter at hand. I have given this exercise to probably 90% of my psychotherapy clients, and many of them have come back to me and expressed how liberating it is to be able to practice something that allows them to not get so thrown off track by the thoughts in their mind. Hopefully over time, you will be able to achieve the same sort of success with this technique. You will have that damn nagging thought in the back of your mind that you have ruined things beyond repair, AND you will be able to quickly switch your attention back to taking those actions that will help you move forward in your quest.

Speaking of moving forward in your quest... you deserve it. You deserve to move onward and upward. Another stumbling block that has been expressed to me by many people is the feeling that moving on or letting go would somehow be wrong,

68

because it would imply that you are pretending like all the shit that happened in the past didn't actually happen. What an impossible situation. No wonder you feel hopeless! You can't move on from the past, and you also can't handle living with the past every day? That sucks. I think people frequently come up against this challenge when they have hit a crisis point. It can be really hard to move on from the weight of the past when you're telling yourself that so many of the things that you did or didn't do during that time contributed to the crisis that you find yourself in right now. It's a nasty negative feedback loop of guilt. You feel bad for getting in this situation and the guilt makes it hard to get out of the situation. Furthermore, sometimes at a certain level you feel that you even deserve to be in this situation due to those actions or inactions. I have a strategy that can be useful for this incredibly frustrating scenario.

Have you ever heard the term "emotional bankruptcy?" I've heard it a few times before in different contexts. Usually when people use it, they refer to the state of being nearly void of emotions due to having been hurt too many times. Someone who is an empty shell of their previous emotional self.

I think of it in a **very different** way. I think of emotional bankruptcy as a viable option for allowing you to cut your losses and move forward with your life, even though you have built up a great deal of baggage in the form of guilt and other emotions. In the world of finances, bankruptcy is there as an option that is available when you accumulate more debt than you can reasonably manage. Basically, the government agrees to absolve your debt, with some repercussions. It's not just a blank slate. You still take a hit and have some negative consequences that will definitely remind you that you let things get out of hand. The great thing about it is that it also allows you to move on. It may not be a blank slate, but it's an opportunity for a new start. In my weird little brain, I think it can be extremely useful for some people who are experiencing depression to declare emotional bankruptcy.

This technique is helpful for those of you who just feel SO burdened by the past that you can't even begin to move forward. Like I mentioned above, we can sometimes feel crushed under the weight of our own guilt. How fucked up is that? We are trying to move forward, and the fact that we haven't been able to move forward until this point is the very thing keeping us feeling guilty and preventing us from moving forward at all. If this applies to you, I want you to consider declaring emotional bankruptcy. You can't ever deny all of the things that have lead you to this point, but it is absolutely certain that you won't be able to improve if they are constantly overwhelming you. **I hereby absolve you of your emotional debt.** You don't have to find a way to mentally reconcile every single action or inaction. I know you try. As if there were some way to think about it long enough to figure out a way to feel less shitty about it. OR you might be the type to just replay scenarios in your head over and over, as a sort of self-flagellation, because, in your mind, you deserve exactly what has happened. I call bullshit. The past is not the present. Yes, it has influenced what you are going through, but if you let it stay in the past, it will stop hurting you so badly in the present.

This is not a perfect solution. In a perfect world, you would never have to deal with this crap. I wish that were the case. Second best is to move forward from it and work on crafting a life that works *for* you and not *against* you. That doesn't mean that you are dodging responsibility for your mistakes. In some ways, you are finally giving yourself the chance to stand up to them, acknowledge your part, and then do the responsible thing of trying to better yourself by moving forward for the sake of you and everyone around you.

You owe it to yourself to move forward. Imagine the advice that you might give to a friend in a similar situation. I'm sure that you would be WAY more gracious with them. You would tell them that it sucks that things have gotten all fucked up AND you know they can get through it if they leave the past in the past. Extend that same grace to yourself. You deserve it just as much as anyone else. Imagine everything that has happened so far will be a really crazy story to tell someone over a beer one day. You WILL look back on this as a learning experience. Let's stop being such a jerk to you so we can get you closer to that point of looking back in the rearview mirror at all of this. You don't need to keep all of your mistakes or all of the pain that others have caused you right in the forefront of your mind. It's nothing that you aren't already aware of. Let it fade into the background while you continue to focus on the stuff that you DO have control over. You got this.

That whole looking back scenario can also serve as the basis for another helpful activity. Imagine sitting with a friend over a beer, coffee, or whatever equivalent situation comes to mind. Picture yourself in the future. Don't be particular about the details. It's just been enough time for this difficult period to be a memory that you can reflect on. As you sit there with your friend, you tell the story of all of the crazy shit that happened and how it all contributed to you feeling really upset, sad, and hopeless. This is a story of triumph, though. You also tell them about how you were able to overcome some of your personal demons and the roadblocks that were keeping you at a standstill. You tell them about the lessons you learned along the way. Don't be shy about dropping some knowledge on this friend. You learned these lessons the hard way. I encourage you to get out a piece of paper and actually write this narrative down, or even speak it out loud to the voice memo thingy on your phone as if you were literally talking to that friend.

There is actually some magic to this technique. Writing from this future perspective is great, because it forces you to automatically adopt the assumption that you are capable of getting through the muck that you currently find yourself knee-deep in. You can upload some of the burden onto the pages of your journal and relieve a few pounds of that heavy pack you carry all of your worries and regrets in. Like before, I don't want you to think for one second that I am asking you to be blindly optimistic. I don't roll like that. Essentially, this is a visualization exercise, and visualization exercises seem to be much more effective when we are realistic. Don't imagine that you are suddenly a superhero with thick skin that is impervious to the stupid offhand comments that gnaw at your self-confidence. Don't imagine that you one day found all of the motivation in the world to complete every single project you had previously abandoned. Instead, imagine yourself struggling. That's right. Imagine that you had to put up the fight of your life against this crap, but you did it. You got through it one way or another. Visualize yourself putting in the work and learning all of the lessons that come along with enrolling in the School of Hardknocks. I'm talking Rocky-style montages of getting your ass kicked over and over while you learn the best ways to rise above each setback. In the end, you get to look back on this period of progress and shake your head at how fucking wild it was. Maybe you can even laugh a little bit at how it simultaneously feels so far away and like it was just yesterday that you were having such a hard time. Emotionally, it feels miles away. That is a great feeling to have. You will get there. I mean it.

Ch. 6 Let's Get Physical

Depression is a sneaky little asshole. One aspect of depression that is vitally important to understand is that it is not always what it seems. If you are feeling very surprised by the symptoms that you are having, especially if the pieces don't seem to add up, you might be experiencing depression caused by some other primary issue. Unfortunately, there are a ton of things that can mimic depression by causing symptoms that are very similar or identical.

In a differential diagnosis, which is something that you need to leave to us professionals (we need jobs too), it is always important to consider the possibility that the depressive symptoms are better explained by some other factor. This does NOT mean that the strategies and advice in this book will not be helpful for you. I just want to make sure that you aren't off relentlessly pursuing a false trail while you investigate the source of why you are feeling so poorly. There are really a ton of potential sources for your depressive symptoms that could be right under your nose. I won't be able to cover all of them here, but I want to give you some of the categories and specific issues that I have most often come across during my professional work as a psychologist. Let me please reiterate that this is not an exhaustive list and you should ask your doctor about any and all potential sources of your depressive symptoms.

The first thing to mention on this list is medication. Medication is awesome. It can help you with so many different medical issues, including depression. However, as we say in the biz, there is no such thing as a biochemical free lunch. In other words, we haven't found a way to eradicate all medication side effects yet. Aside from weight gain and sexual dysfunction, one of the most annoying side effects is ... you guessed it: depression. Some of the medications that can cause depression are pretty intuitive. For instance, anticonvulsant medications, which are the type of medications that you use to treat seizure disorders, can definitely have depression as a side effect. When you think about what it would take to prevent seizures, it makes a lot of sense. You are basically trying to bring your nervous system down a few notches so that you stop having electrical storms going off in your brain. When you try to slow down the activity in your brain, a side effect is sometimes feeling slowed down in other ways, which can look a whole lot like depression. Many other medications such as Accutane for acne, blood pressure medications, and contraceptives can also have depressive symptoms among their potential side effects.

Don't let this freak you out and make you stop taking all of your medications. Actually, definitely don't do that before you check with your doctor. It's important to realize that just because a medication has depression as a potential side effect, that doesn't automatically mean that it's the culprit. Side effects are listed in a pretty conservative manner. Basically, the drug companies want to make sure their asses are covered, so if a certain number of people report a given side effect during the research trials, they include it as a potential side effect (just so you can't say they didn't warn you). This means that side effects, like depressive symptoms, are not always present when taking a given medication. The important thing here is to go to your doctor and rule it out. (I need to repeat myself here because I know that I am speaking to the WebMD self-diagnosis generation. Don't just decide to go off of a medication on your own because you read that depressive symptoms might be a side effect for some people. Work through the process with your medical doctor. Ruling out medication side effects is absolutely a vital part of any good differential diagnosis for depression, but it needs to be done carefully. One good aspect of living in an age of oversaturation when it comes to pharmaceuticals is that there are often many different options for any given medical issue. Your doctor might switch your blood pressure or anticonvulsant medication to one of a different variety. After that point, if your depression persists, you have more data that supports the hypothesis of that depression being due issues other than medication.)

Physical conditions, diseases, and syndromes can also cause symptoms that are remarkably similar to those seen in depression. One of the most common disorders that can mimic depression is hypothyroidism. I have seen this many times in my professional work; people who have things pretty well sorted out, but just cannot shake the icky symptoms of depression that cloud their everyday life. The thyroid is a gland in the body that produces important hormones for regulating normal functioning. When the thyroid gets out of whack, it is really a huge pain in the ass. (There are many different potential causes of thyroid dysfunction, which I will not go into here because it's not my area of specialty.) Basically, you can have an overactive thyroid, which is called *hyper*thyroidism, or an underactive thyroid, which is called *hypo*thyroidism. I said the thyroid is a pain in the ass because the symptoms of hyperthyroidism basically look very similar to anxiety and the symptoms of hypothyroidism look very similar to depression. Some of the common symptoms of an underactive thyroid are fatigue, poor concentration, and weight gain with poor appetite. Going back to the diagnostic symptoms of depression, I'm sure you can see how this might get confusing. Luckily, thyroid issues are pretty easy to diagnose. I know that I sound like a broken record, but let's again utilize our medical doctors for this. Typically if you have questions about your thyroid function, your doc will send you to an endocrinologist who specializes in looking at hormonal functioning in the body. If there is an issue there, they will be able to identify it and suggest possible treatments to help out. In my personal experience, I have had therapy patients resolve most of their depressive symptoms after going on medication to regulate their thyroid functioning. Just like every other physical source of depressive symptoms I mention in this chapter, thyroid issues will not be the golden ticket for everyone. Getting some synthetic thyroid hormone medication will not help you manage your depression if your thyroid is actually functioning normally in the first place. So get a medical workup and continue the diagnostic process of ruling these things out.

Aside from thyroid dysfunction, there are quite a few other disorders that can cause symptoms of depression. Problems with blood sugar, such as diabetes, can have an effect on energy level, motivation, irritability, and all of that good stuff. There are also autoimmune diseases such as Grave's disease, anemia, lupus (insert House M.D. joke), Celiac disease, and Crohn's disease, which can contribute to your depressive symptoms. There seems to be some link (that we are still figuring out) between the chronic inflammation that is common in autoimmune disorders and depression, so if you got the short end of the stick with one of these disorders, that is another place to look for the root of your depressive symptomology.

When I was in grade school and we learned all about drugs, I remember them basically being characterized as uppers or downers. Cocaine, meth, and things like that are uppers because they excite your nervous system and get you raging hard. Heroine, benzos, weed, and alcohol are downers because they slow down your central nervous system and get you super chilled. Another name for downers are depressants, because they depress the arousal and stimulation levels within your nervous system. So, if you are regularly deciding to ingest depressants and then get surprised that you are feeling depressed ... you're gonna have a bad time. Seriously though, people often neglect to recognize the impact of the things that you ingest on your mood and physiology.

If you have rampant anxiety, it's probably a good idea to lay off the coffee. If you are a depressed person, you should probably be careful with the booze. Think of it like a threshold similar to water's temperature. With water, you reach a certain threshold temperature and you start to boil - that is kind of like anxiety, where you get more and more worked up until you feel downright anxious or even have a panic attack. On the flip side, you also have the freezing point of water, where once you dip below that point things start getting slower and slower until they freeze entirely. That's like depression. Once you dip below that threshold, you start to feel legitimate depressive symptoms like lethargy, painful feelings of sadness, and a sense of being hopeless. By putting depressants like alcohol into your body, you are basically starting yourself off a few steps closer to that threshold. That means it only takes one or two shitty things to set you off on the path of feeling really lousy and depressed. While you may still be susceptible to depression without the alcohol, you would at least have a little more of a buffer before reaching that threshold. Does this mean that you can't ever have some alcohol? Of course not. It's just something to keep in mind. Sometimes having a beer with a friend and talking about life can be really helpful for your mood. Other times, when you have a few drinks, you are basically setting yourself up to feel sad by giving your depression a kickstart.

Know thyself and don't be stubborn. I know that drugs are fun ... that's the whole point. Just don't pretend that it doesn't make a difference. It's something that personally pisses me off when people with anxiety are like, "Oh, caffeine doesn't do anything to me. I can drink an espresso and go straight to sleep!" Or when people with depression are like, "Man, I can put down a 6 pack and not feel a thing. That's definitely not what's making me feel lazy. I've written a whole paper after drinking before!" Gahh! Sorry for getting a little aggro, but it drives me crazy. It's not like a willpower sort of thing. These substances were designed to directly have an effect on your nervous system. That's their whole point. You're lying to yourself if you say that they don't make a difference. Sure, you can have a tolerance. Bodies are great at habituating to things, but that doesn't mean the substance suddenly becomes inactive. Again, I'm not saying don't drink or whatever it is you kids do these days. Shit, I'm sipping a beautiful glass of Basil

Hayden's as I write this. Just like my advice in pretty much every other chapter in this book. Be <u>realistic</u>.

I listen to a lot of podcasts as a means to feed my hungry multitasking brain. As I'm writing this chapter, some words that I heard from Joe Rogan (yes the comedian that commentates the UFC fights) keep popping into my head. He said, "The people that I know who have the hardest time emotionally are people that don't work out. And the people that I know that do work out, especially the ones that work out hard, they expel these big giant bursts of energy where your body is like almost dying, you're heaving, your heart is pounding in your chest, you're barely able to lift this piece of metal up again, you're barely able to jump up on this box again, and by putting yourself in that intense form of stress, it makes regular life more peaceful." Now Joe is on the extreme side of this camp. I'm certainly not practicing what he preaches every day. I do exercise, but I'm not pushing myself to vomit peak every day. Though I can say that the times when I have pushed myself that hard have indeed brought about some very special mental clarity.

The point that I want to make here is that exercise is **vitally** important when it comes to regulating your mood. It's almost as important as it is for losing weight. If you're overweight, the first thing that will be suggested is to start exercising more than you do now. Really, the same thing can go for depression. It's not that running or lifting weights is going to change the deep down structure of your thoughts and how you interpret the world, but it absolutely will change the way that your emotions hit you. If something negative happens and you are working from a physically lethargic, sedentary baseline, it's going to feel like an emotional kick in the balls, and your day and/or week will be ruined. If you are taking good care of your body by pushing yourself to exercise regularly, it seems to be that you can build up a bit of a buffer so the same negative event doesn't hit you as hard, and you are still able to do the things that you want to accomplish. I know this is probably not news for you, but I really want you to take a moment to recognize how awesome this is. There are so many things in depression that are confusing, and it's so hard to figure out what you could possibly do to make change. It can feel like almost everything is out of your control. This is one thing that you have direct influence over. You can actually do something that is scientifically proven to have a direct effect on your mood. How badass is that?

Of course, with depression it is not as simple as flipping the switch and turning into a fitness god. The good thing is that you don't have to. Motivation is definitely at play here. It is MEGA hard to go from feeling like a useless lump to getting off your ass and moving your body a bit. I won't retread all the things I mentioned in the motivation chapter, but I want to talk about a few things you can do to overcome any roadblocks that stand in the way of your exercising.

First off, you don't need to start huge. The idea of exercising can be quite imposing, but it doesn't have to be. It's not a competition, and no one else gives a shit what you are doing for exercise. Just start at a place that makes sense for you. Maybe that means that you are taking a nice long walk while you listen to your favorite podcasts, albums, or audiobooks a few times per week. Maybe you have a gym membership you can finally put to use. Even if you go to the gym 3 times per week for just 30 minutes, you are still going to have a positive impact on your mental and physical health. I know it feels like people are judging you for not diving in headfirst and going hard on the bench press, screaming with all of your might while you crank out an Olympic feat of strength. They aren't. Instead of focusing on the end goal, just focus on doing more than you are now.

If there is any way to integrate some pleasure and reward from the exercise, that will help even more! For instance, some people might hate the idea of going for a run around the neighborhood with every fiber of their being. Maybe something like dancing would be less boring. Instead of forcing yourself to run aimlessly around town, try going to a Zumba class and shaking your ass off to the beat of some fun-thumping music. You can likely go to a free beginner's class at any number of gyms, fitness centers, or dance studios around you.

Maybe you're not the dancing type? How about an opportunity to beat the crap out of something and get praised for it? There has probably never been a better time to get into martial arts. With the rise in popularity of mixed martial arts, there are more opportunities than ever to try it out. Again, you can try out a sample class at any number of places around you. MMA was my exercise of choice all throughout college.

Each gym certainly has its own personality. Some places you go are full of douchebag meatheads, but other places have a bunch of lovely people like yourself, just trying to get out there and do something vigorous with their bodies. That's the good thing about free samples; you can try it before you buy it. Group classes like these are great because you can totally lose track of time as you pick up on the excitement and motivation of your fellow ass kickers/shakers. There are any number of cool classes or activities out there. You can hike, kayak, play soccer, pick up free running, hula hoop, soul cycle, or whatever the hell gets you excited. The point is that if you are able to get excited and actually *enjoy* the activities that you engage in, you are going to train yourself to enjoy being more active in general. Get out there and have some fun, damn it!

Sometimes, we actually have legitimate excuses for not exercising. Physical disabilities, illnesses, and all of that other fun stuff can really limit your ability to do all of those things that I talked about before. While that definitely sucks, there are things you can do about it. If you have physical limitations like arthritis, asthma, etc. that inhibit your ability to participate in high impact activities, you might have a look at swimming or underwater exercise. It's not just for old people (though it's GREAT for old people). While it is low impact, swimming is still a great source of cardiovascular exercise, which makes it a perfect candidate for improving your mood. If you are thinking about attending a fitness class and are afraid that it might be too intense for you, simply take a minute to talk to the instructor before the class starts. They will let you know the best ways that you can participate in the class given your limitations and will mostly likely be super excited to have the challenge of trying to adapt the class to fit all different ability and activity levels. Have you ever seen wheelchair basketball or wheelchair Zumba? It's freakin' awesome. There is almost always a way for you to get out there and spike your heart rate a few times per week while having fun with it. If you need to do it a different way, that is okay. Don't be afraid to ask for help or options. They are out there. And remember... no one gives a shit about what you are doing because they are just trying to focus on not keeling over and dying themselves.

The final thing that I want to mention about exercise is it's a great way to meet new people and maybe even make friends. The topic of making friends as an adult is something that has come up many times with patients of mine. How the hell are you supposed to just go and make friends when you don't have school or something like that to make the process automatic? Well, exercise classes are a great place to do that when you don't want to find people at work or at the bar. There are so many good things about this. Not only are friends great because they are extending your personal network of support and allies, but these people that you will likely run into at these sorts of activities are probably going to be interested in bettering themselves as well. That means you're on the same quest and can help one another to be more motivated to follow through with your goals. The buddy system works!

Of course no chapter on physical contributors to depression would be complete without addressing diet a little bit. I am not a dietician. Therefore, I am not going to pretend like I know the exact diet that you should be following. It is important that you are eating well, though.

As you know, it doesn't take much to throw you off your game when you are depressed. Anything that we can do to minimize your chances of feeling like shit is a good thing. That means that you want to make sure that your diet is providing you with enough readily available energy to take action when you are able to capture some elusive motivation. Inadequate nutrition can also contribute to feelings of lethargy and fatigue. If these are issues for you, check in with your doctor. You will want to make sure that allergies or sensitivities are not keeping your body in a constant state of drain. In my opinion, you don't need to jump the gun and dive into paleo or some other bullshit fad diet. Just try to become more aware of the ways in which your dietary choices impact your physical and emotional state.

If you are quite overweight, you don't need me to tell you that losing some weight can help. Gaining weight can be a symptom and a contributor to depression. By that I mean you can put on weight due to your feelings of sadness and gaining weight can also make those feelings of sadness worse. It's probably an all-around good idea to shed some of that gained weight. Along with exercise, the right diet can really help out with that. If you have the means to do so, go see a dietician and have them do the hard work for you. They can analyze your current eating behaviors and suggest some changes that may have a significant impact on your mood and energy level.

Sleep is the last thing that I want to talk about in this chapter. Sleep is an interesting one because, much like weight gain, it can be both a symptom and a cause. Hypersomnia (sleeping too much) or insomnia (trouble falling asleep) are both symptoms of a major depressive episode. Not getting enough sleep can also be something that throws your body off and causes you to feel out of sorts. It can sometimes be disruptive enough of your mood on its own that you start to feel depressed from not sleeping well. As with everything else, I will encourage you to check in with your doctor if you are having consistent issues with sleep. They might make you do some tests to make sure there isn't something like sleep apnea or some other sleeping disorder going on that's to blame for your poor sleep. Beyond that, there are a few tips I can share for helping you to be a better sleeper, which can in turn help regulate your mood and get you to wake up on the *right* side of the bed every once in a while.

The practices and habits that help to promote good sleep are collectively referred to as sleep hygiene. There are a few sleep hygiene basics that you should probably have in your back pocket. Hopefully I've gotten across already that your brain is pretty powerful. It has this amazing ability to learn new things and make associations that can sometimes help us and sometimes hinder us. Take a moment to think of the things that you do in bed. Ideally there are only two things that you should be doing in bed. One of them is sleeping. What else do you do? Do you find yourself using your laptop in bed to complete work? Check your email? Do you watch your favorite shows in bed? Each of these things could potentially be wrecking your sleep. It comes down to association.

You ever hear the story of Pavlov's dogs? Basically, this dude wanted to mess with some dogs, so he started ringing a bell every time he presented them with delicious food. Over time, he noticed that the dogs would salivate at the sound of the bell even when there wasn't actually food present. It's the same reason that your pets come running like a bat out of hell when you open up a bag of chips for yourself. They think that it is a treat for them. They made the association between the sound of crinkling and the receiving of delicious treats. So when you continually pair the location of your bed with the process of doing work, or the entertainment of watching television, you weaken the association that your brain has between bed and sleep. Also GET YOUR DAMN PHONE OUT OF THE BEDROOM. If your tiny little bright white screen is the last thing that you look at before you go to sleep and the first thing that you look at when you wake up... you're doing it wrong. They still make alarm clocks that are only meant to serve as alarm clocks... I suggest you use that instead.

Reading is a tricky one. I think that reading in bed can be okay, but it is very personal and subjective. For some people, reading non-fiction books like biographies, self-help books, or informational books gets their brain too amped and motivated to go kick ass. Not always conducive to sleep. For others, reading something that is more bland and informational can help to lull them off to sleep. Use your personal judgment for this, and keep being a good scientist by engaging in trial and error. If you change or remove your bedtime reading, take notice of the effect that it has on your sleep and act accordingly. The jury is still out on whether using devices can interrupt sleep just due to the type of light that they give off. Personally, I think you don't really need to worry about that aspect of it as much as the accidental associations I just described. If you want to be safe, just read your book, whether it be physical or on an E-reader, in a different room than the one in which you sleep. Think of it as a treat to yourself. Find a nice comfy nook in the front room or wherever looks nice you, make a nice cup of herbal tea, and curl up for a few minutes to read. When you find that your eyes can't take it anymore and you are ready to pass out, stumble your way over to the bed and PTFO.

Really the most helpful action that you can take in regards to sleep hygiene is to do the same thing nearly every night. If you do the reading nook wind-down like I just described, do that each night. If you play a game on your iPad (like me), play the same one every night, and only play that game before sleep. Basically, you want to create a consistent winding down sequence at the end of the night, so that each step along the way, your body gets more and more tired as it anticipates the lovely sleep you're about to have. Even if you can't make it to bed at the same exact time every night, your body should know that when you start the first activity of your wind down sequence, it can expect to be snoring in about 30 minutes.

So that's really all I would like to mention in regards to physical considerations for depression. These aren't revolutionary ideas, nor are they a complete list of the things that you should be watching out for. This whole chapter was basically a way for me to introduce a few broad categories of things you might have overlooked in your quest to determine the source of your depression. They are annoying, but they are also great in that once you start to pay attention to these sources of depressive symptoms, you can often make huge strides toward feeling much better. And even if these are not the main culprits for your unique brand of depression, it certainly doesn't hurt any to exercise more, drink less, sleep well, and eat better. In fact, you might find that the process of going through trial and error to identify causes can help you feel like you have more control and agency over your life. And it can propel you forward as you defeat this monster.

Ch. 7 A Letter to Those Who Don't Understand Depression

Not knowing what to say to other people about your depression is totally understandable. If this is a struggle for you, you're most certainly not the only one. Aside from the nearly impossible task of explaining what it feels like to have depression, it's also super difficult to ask your friends and family for help. Even when you do work up the courage to ask them for help, how the hell are you supposed to know what to tell them when they ask you how they can be supportive?

Society is flooded with misconceptions about depression. We are constantly bombarded with the message that we should be thankful, motivated, and happy because of all that we have in life. We are told that we should be able to easily shake off adversity to continue on our paths. It's no wonder people give such terrible advice when they hear that you are depressed. It can be frustrating and exhausting to try to explain it to people. All of the effort that you have at your disposal is being spent on keeping yourself afloat while you struggle through this. Sometimes it just feels like too much to bother trying to make someone understand. This can lead to irritation and telling people things like "I'm fine", "Don't worry about it", or "Never mind". I want to try to ease this burden for you a little bit.

One thing that I added into the 2nd edition of F**k Anxiety was a letter to people who don't "get it" when it comes to anxiety. The feedback that I got about the letter was overwhelmingly positive, so I thought that I would give it a shot again. In what follows, I will do my best to put myself in the headspace of someone who lives with depression and write a letter to someone that might not quite understand what you are going through. I will write through this letter off the top of my head and then come back and discuss different pieces of it to see what suggestions I might be able to offer for talking to people about your depression or asking others for help.

Dear _____,

You are getting this letter because you are an important person in my life, and I want you to understand more about what I'm going through. I know that I can be difficult and I'm sorry for that. I know that I probably don't need to be sorry, but I am. In fact, I feel guilty for feeling sorry in the first place. Ridiculous, I know. That's how my brain works because I have depression... and yes, my mind is an exhausting place. I want to give you this letter to help you understand a little more about what I am going through, ask for some grace as I work this crap out, and to suggest a few ways that you can best support me if you are willing.

The first thing I want you to know is that I am trying. Or, rather ... I am trying to try. You see, 1 and 1 don't always add up to 2 with depression. There are legitimate biological differences between me and someone who doesn't live with depression, which makes this a really difficult uphill battle. I am literally fighting against my biology which tries to tell me that none of this is worth it and that I shouldn't even try. When people say things like, "Just think positively," or "It's all in your head," it does not help at all. I know it's in my head, but unfortunately it is not as easy as flipping a switch and suddenly feeling better. I know that probably have 1000 reasons to be happy, and sometimes I feel like the worst person ever for being so down all the time despite them.

Fighting off depression is not a simple task. If it was, I would have done it already. Trust me when I say that I am so tired of feeling like crap all of the time. I am actively trying to take steps to better myself and steal some of my life back from this depressive monster that has crept in like a black cloud raining over all of my thoughts and feelings. The process will involve challenging my negative thought patterns, pushing myself to re-engage with things that I used to enjoy, working to forgive myself for letting things get so out of hand, and finding people that I trust to be on my team. That's why you are reading this. I want you to be on my team. I know that I have not been the easiest person to be around recently. Maybe my actions or inactions have even hurt you in some way. The thing is, I need support to dig myself out of these patterns. I don't need a yes or no answer from you right now, but I want to share a few things that do and do not help me in case you are ever willing to lend a hand.

For now, this has to be on my terms. I am feeling more broken and fragile than I would like to admit. Down the line, I might need a bit of a push, but for now, tough love is not what I need. That means that unsolicited advice that worked for you or someone else is probably not helpful. Unfortunately, there is no one size fits all approach to depression. It's a very individualized sort of beast. Also, being told that what I am going through is not that bad is very hurtful for me. I know that it might not be logical for me to feel this way given my life circumstances. I know it could be worse and that there are many others in the world who have it worse. That's just how depression works. Intellectually knowing something and feeling it are two very different experiences. I'm working to make them more in sync.

Though my instinct tells me otherwise, it's probably not the best idea for me to be alone all of the time right now. So, please have a little grace and forgiveness with me if I get irritated or act in off-putting ways. I do want you to be here, and I really appreciate you continuing to try. I feel like a lot of people have given up on me. I don't want you to be one of them.

Probably the most helpful thing that you can do for me is to let me know that you are here. I forget sometimes, so please don't assume that I already know. Tell me that you are here if I need you. I won't always know the best ways that you can help me, and you don't have to either. I mostly just need to know that I'm not on this journey alone.

Like I said, a big part of this process of recovery is finding ways to fight back against these unhelpful patterns of thinking that I have fallen into. Sometimes, it can be really helpful to have someone that I can rely on as a "logical barometer." Basically, I can tell you what my train of thought is regarding a situation, and you can tell me whether you think it makes sense or not. You can share how you, as a non-depressed person, might interpret it. That helps me to practice reeling in the overgeneralizing, personalizing, and overall amplification of negative thoughts. My thoughts usually start out rooted in reality, but they get way blown out of proportion, and you could definitely help me out by nonjudgmentally letting me know how far off my thinking has gone. You don't have to be "right" to help me out with this. There are really no right or wrong answers, but I will be much better off if I have a few people that I can get input from when I am doubting my initial interpretation of things.

I am trying to do more. This might mean that I am trying to get back to doing things that I used to enjoy, because everything feels very bland right now. It also might mean that I am trying to get off of my butt and be more physically active. It is so incredibly hard to find the motivation inside myself to do these things. One change that can give me more motivation to follow through with plans is when I have a buddy to do them along with me. Maybe you could be that person. I don't mean that you need to do everything with me, but if there is something that you enjoy that I might benefit from, maybe consider inviting me along. Speaking of inviting me along, I won't always say yes. Even if it is something as simple as going to dinner or the movies, sometimes it feels like the weight of my symptoms are literally crushing me, and I will pass on almost any invitation. Please keep inviting me. You don't need to waste all of your time *trying to convince me, just don't give up on me. Keep offering, please.*

Finally, I would be so grateful if you would help other people understand what I am going through. Hopefully at this point, you "get it" a little more. Depression is something that we are told to keep a secret, and it is really hard for me to share my feelings sometimes. You are reading this letter because I trust you and want you to be on my team. It is exhausting for me to reach out to each person and ask for help, so if you could help other friends and family understand when they ask what is wrong with me, I would really appreciate it.

If you are reading this far, that means that I was right about you. You are amazing and a perfect addition to my depression fighting team. Like I said before, I really am trying. This is a tough battle, and I don't know how long it will take, but having allies like you will certainly make the process that much easier. I am not asking for a blank slate. I know that I can sometimes say or do things that make me not so pleasant to be around. That's the nature of the beast. You are allowed to be upset, angry, hurt, or annoyed at those things. I just ask that you try to understand that these things are an expression of my depressive symptoms. They may be a part of me, but they are not the whole me. I hope this letter helps you to understand a little more about the other part of me that is dying for a chance to get out into the world.

Sincerely,

_____

PS: Please feel free to ask questions. I'm sure this is a lot to take in. It's not the easiest thing to explain. I may not always have the answers for you, but you are welcome to ask.

Like I said, that was basically off the top of my head. I hope that I covered some things that resonated with you here. It's impossible to encapsulate the experience of each and every one of you, because depression is such a personal and individual experience. This was based on my professional and personal experiences, so forgive me if I missed a few things. As I look back on the letter, I can see a few areas that are worth mentioning.

Trust me, I understand that people suck at helping. I hear about it all the time. People tend to give plain and simple advice that worked for someone else or that they heard about on some television show, as if you had not already considered those strategies. It's not entirely their fault they are bad at helping. It just means that they have not had the pleasure of diving head first into the dark pool of depression like you have. They are the lucky ones. Pardon their ignorance in the same way that you would like them to pardon some of your behaviors. These people are legitimately trying to be helpful. There are just such strong differences between someone who is in the thick of depression and someone who is not, it can feel like you are speaking a different language. By speaking with them about what you are going through or giving them a letter like this one, you can provide them tools to work with. Send me to go help someone repair their motorcycle, I will be more than willing, but will probably cause more issues by helping in the wrong way. If you give me a tool and teach me a specific way to use it, I can actually make a difference. This is the same thing. You can recruit people to be a part of your team and give them a particular role to fill.

Though they will never be able to understand exactly what it feels like for you to be going through depression, you might be able to give them an approximation. Usually, it helps to relate it to something they may have experienced in their life. Provided that you are talking to an adult, it is pretty likely that they have experienced some sort of loss before. Whether it be the loss of a family member, the loss of a pet, or the loss of their dream job, they were probably "not themselves" during the period of time following the loss. They were experiencing a normal and healthy grief reaction, but it probably looked a bit similar to the depression that you feel. Even though a certain part of their brain knew that everything could be okay, they were just not in a place where they could think logically and reasonably yet. They probably felt a bit hopeless about the whole situation. Maybe they got hit hard with the more overt emotional symptoms like crying spells or that anhedonia feeling of blandness that we talked about. Whatever their particular brand of grief looked like, I'm sure they can agree that it felt like the wind was taken out of their sails for a while. Ask them to try and imagine that those icky feelings that they had at the time were their baseline. Tell them that is what an average day feels like, and when actual negative things happen, it amps up the pain, hopelessness, and emptiness even more.

If you are the type to have a more agitated, angry, or irritable sort of depression, maybe you can relate it to the feeling of road rage. We have all been pissed at someone who is driving like a jackass and completely cuts us off on the highway. You know that the encounter is over and you should let it go, but it just feels impossible. You are practically stewing in your anger and irritation. How could you possibly just let it go? UGH. There are some universal experiences that most everyone can relate to. Fortunately for most people, these are the exception and not the rule. Unfortunately for you, this is how you feel the majority of the time and that is why you are so sick of being this way.

It's also important for me to mention that you are allowed to have feelings. Just because the way you feel might be a bit over dramatic or exaggerated, it doesn't mean your feelings aren't real. It will be important for you to find your own personal balance between asking for grace and forgiveness for your behaviors from those around you and being assertive with them about your right to own your feelings and pain. It all comes down to your particular situation. If the people you are talking to are part of the problem and you think it's just because they don't understand, help them to "get it." Show them how what they have done in the past is not helpful for you, and tell them some ways that they can be better. If they're part of the problem and seem to legitimately not give a shit, they may not be worth your effort. I'm sorry that you have to deal with such negativity in your life, but sometimes admitting to yourself that certain people will not change (even though they are hurting you) is a necessary step in the journey of overcoming depression.

These tips that I have given will not be the golden ticket for everyone. You can most certainly pick and choose what I have laid out for you. Maybe there are some parts that definitely resonate with you. I welcome you to use those parts and ignore the other stuff that might not fit so well. You are more than welcome to use this letter word-for-word in its entirety if you'd like. I'll provide a free downloadable version on my website at duffthepsych.com/depressionletter that you can print off. Otherwise, you can use bits and pieces of it as inspiration for your own letter, email, video, conversation, or any format that will be most helpful to you.

Ch. 8 Be Nice to Future You

This chapter is not going to cover one specific issue related to depression. Instead, I want to talk about a broad underlying concept that can really amp up your asskickery. In my observation of people who live with depression, they are able to make much greater gains when they not only work hard at their recovery, but also work smart. Smarter? Smartly? Whatever. This chapter is all about ways to set yourself up for success. One of the things that I really want to inspire you to do is to maximize your head starts and opportunities and minimize your roadblocks and pitfalls. As I continue to mention, depression is tough. You wouldn't be here if climbing your way out of depression was simple. You need every advantage you can get, but more often than not, you probably fall into patterns that actually work against you and make it more difficult to improve. For instance, you might have highs and lows in your mood. When you are feeling great, you probably don't think too much about your depression or the work that you need to do, because you want to relish that feeling of being somewhat normal again right? Well, it can be nice to reconnect with normality and allow yourself to just sit in that feeling, but it can also serve you really well to use that time to your advantage.

Which brings me to my first tip: use motivation when you have it. When I say motivation, I suppose that is only one aspect of it. Really, I mean those moments of relief where your depression isn't crushing you at full force. This may seem a bit obvious, but time and time again I see people who do not make good use of these opportunities and end up stuck in their progress. Here's a common scenario that I've seen play out in therapy. Someone comes in for a follow up session and they tell me something like this: "Well… I was kind of worried about coming in today, because I'm afraid I don't have much progress to report. It's hard! When I left session with you last week I was energized and motivated. I felt like I was for sure going to make progress this week and put all of those things that we talked about into action… but I just didn't. It was almost hard for me to even remember what we talked about or what it felt like to have that little spark of motivation once I got home and fell back into the normal groove of things. I'm sorry. I feel super guilty." Does that sound like you? That's the depressive mindset right there.

We can break this down a little bit and see the areas where this hypothetical person is not quite setting themselves up for success as much as they could be. The first thing to recognize is that this is probably not new. As much as it pains me to say, a person who comes into session with this type of news has probably said the same thing in previous weeks. Here's the common pattern; you have a spike in energy, motivation, and normality following something positive, such as a therapy session, followed by a drop off as the cosmic force of depression begins to draw you back into its icy clutches. If you notice a pattern like this somewhere in your life, whether it be after a therapy session, a meal, or just a good talk with a friend, **use** that pattern to your advantage. How awesome is it that you can pretty reliably know a time in your life when you have a greater capacity to make changes? Think of that momentary relief as a golden opportunity to set yourself up for success. What are the things you have a hard time doing when you feel most oppressed by your depression? Do those things during this time window.

I had one person patient who really benefitted from working on their journal, thought log, or other "homework" activities from session right after they left the office, because they knew they would probably avoid it later on. In fact, we worked out a unique arrangement where he would actually go back out to the waiting room and start his journaling before even leaving the building. That helped massively, because there were no opportunities for him to get distracted by something else and lose that motivational boost.

This tip doesn't only apply to the afterglow of special activities. In a normal day, we tend to have a certain ebb and flow to our emotions, energy, and motivation. I would encourage you to notice them. When are your good times? For me, I tend to have a few different good periods throughout the day and my brain, being the troll that it is, doesn't like to put any of those good periods during the work day when I should actually be getting shit done. I bet I'm not alone in that. Just because I tend to have one of my best periods at 11 PM right before bed doesn't mean that hour is useless. I have just learned to capitalize on that good hour as much as I can. I know that it doesn't make too much sense to start up a new project or jump into something taxing, since I am trying to wind down for the day. However, by paying attention to the trends in my life, I know that my mornings are typically some of the worst periods of time for me, in terms of motivation and productivity. I hate to be that guy who is a dick before he gets his coffee... but I totally am. So, what I have learned to do is take that final hour or 30 minutes in my day and make good use of it to set my grumpy, sleepy, zombie-like morning self up for success.

If you took a browse through my journal (don't look through my journal!), you would definitely be able to tell which pages are from those evening peak hours. This is the best time for me to write down reminders to myself, schedule out my day, write my to do list, set out my clothes, put reminders in my calendar, or outline what I want to write the next day. Actually, that's what is happening right now. It is currently morning time on a Monday, which is pretty much the definition of hell for me, but here I am writing a book for you all. That is because last night, when I felt super awesome at 11, I made a loose schedule for my activities today, and then I covered the wall in Post-it notes to make a big outline of this very chapter that I am writing right now. I'm sitting here looking at my wall and the Post-its that say "use motivation when you have it," "notice when your good times are," and "start projects/plan for your week when you feel good." So now, instead of starting my day off by exhausting all of my mental energy on making decisions about what I should be doing, I was able to wake up, brew some strong ass coffee, listen to NPR, and plug away at this chapter that I had outlined last night when I was feeling better. Set your future self up for success in whatever ways you can.

One of the most powerful weapons that you can use in your battle against depression is a consistent routine. When you are depressed, it can feel like every decision takes up 1000% more brain power, and you can get fatigued by simply trying to make a plan and follow through with it. More often than not, that probably just leads you to say "forget it!" and return to doing nothing. Seriously. Don't wait for that magic day when you will suddenly stop procrastinating. Instead, you need to fight back against the dysregulating force of depression by imposing a structure. Positive structure and routine are the worst enemies of depression, because they help you feel more in control. They help regulate your body and mind. They help you avoid that decision fatigue and just get stuff done, simply because that's what you do.

The first thing to look at is sleep. Poor sleeping patterns definitely magnify the effects of depression and help to maintain a state of overall shittiness. Whether you are hardly sleeping at all or sleeping all day, having a consistent sleep schedule is going to help you out. Remember that we need all of the energy that we can get our hands on, because depression is constantly stealing that energy away from you. A roadblock that I have seen frequently in people with depression is falling into a pattern of going to sleep super late and then sleeping in all day, because they feel like they have no reason to wake up. (Like, what is the point if you're just going to do nothing and disappoint people all day, anyway? That's the depression talking.) Even if you feel like you don't have much reason to wake up, you still need to start forcing yourself to. It's a cycle. When you sleep in excessively, you start your day off feeling like a useless slob, and you sure as hell aren't going to proactively make changes for yourself. Start by waking up at the same time everyday. Even if you are having a difficult time falling asleep quickly and you are dead tired in the morning, just pick a time and stick to it. Don't focus so much on making sure you get the same exact number of hours per night. Even if you get to bed a little later by accident, try to wake up at the same time. After a week or so, your body will adapt to the routine and start to regulate itself. Once you start waking up at the same time of day, your day will be opened up to start imposing more structure and routine.

I am a big fan of making your mornings awesome, because that sets you up for the rest of the day. By nature, mornings are tough. The good thing is, you can make a few changes to turn your mornings into something positive. Treat yourself to a really nice launch sequence for your day.

Here's one routine that works really well for me. I don't stick to it 100% every day, but when I am feeling like I need to get back on track and regulate myself, it really helps to follow through with this routine as much as possible. When I wake up, the first thing that I do is hop in the shower. If I can get myself into the shower, I know I'll be able to stay awake. It takes almost no effort to zombie-walk into the shower and start physiologically activating my body. Then, I start my coffee. I have found that coffee brewing is the perfect time period to practice some meditation. I use a French press for my coffee so while the kettle is heating up on the stove, I sit on the couch or on the floor and practice some mindfulness meditation like we talked about in the chapter about letting go. In the event that I accidentally fall asleep (it has definitely happened), the whistle of the kettle will surely wake my lazy ass up. Once coffee is poured, I sit at the table and journal. The journaling helps me to get my mind on track and plan for the day. Finally, I do a little bit of exercise. I usually don't have time for a full power workout, nor do I want to get all sweaty after I already showered, but some pushups, pullups, planks, or squats are usually perfect to get my blood flowing.

Put those pieces together and do the math. If you activate your body, give yourself a private moment to write down anything and everything on your mind, plan your priorities for the day, and gift yourself a few moments of Zen.... do you really think you are going to start the day off on a bad note? Your routine doesn't have to look just like mine. Feel free to rearrange the pieces and add or subtract as you wish. Maybe your secret ingredient is stepping outside first thing and getting some cold fresh air in your lungs. Maybe you need to have a morning dance party with your headphones blasting. Make your morning awesome, and your day will be much more likely to follow suit. The trick is to keep it consistent. This is your routine. You can probably look back on some periods of your life where you weren't as crippled by your depression. Did those times happen to be when you also had a schedule and a reason to wake up and power through the day? Probably. Like I said before, you don't have to adhere to this routine 100% for your entire life. Think of it as a tool. The more unregulated you are feeling, the more you should rely on your routine to set you up and pull you through.

Daily routine doesn't only matter for your mornings. I also like to "bookend" my days by having some structure to my night. I'm not talking about having a boring, predictable life here. You are still allowed to be spontaneous and have variety in your life, but you only have so many units of motivation and decision energy to use throughout the day. If you can count on a useful and predictable routine for the start and the end of your day, you have more of those precious units to spend wisely throughout the day on stuff that matters. At the end of the night, you will be focusing on a very different goal. Where the mornings are devoted to getting your head on straight and your body amped up for the day, the evenings should be about letting go of the day, disconnecting from stress and trouble, and calming down so that you can get some precious sleep and recharge to kick ass the next day.

These days, we are constantly plugged into the world. At the risk of sounding super lame, I think that we are probably too plugged in. Information is great, and it's an amazing gift that you can have all of the information in the world at your fingertips. The problem that the modern depressive faces is regulating the flow of that information. Don't let these machines control your life, man. By unplugging for a while before bed, you give yourself the opportunity to wind down without some dumbass you knew in high school saying something idiotic and infuriating on Twitter. If not Twitter, it could be a work email you stumble across when you decide to refresh just one more time before heading to sleep that gets you all worked up about the next day. It could be any number of things. It doesn't even have to be something that is explicitly upsetting. As you are well aware, the brain of a depressed person is a big asshole and can often take any external stimuli and (by some miraculous process) convert it into something... depressing. I can't speak to your specific version of this super power, but I have heard tales of seeing happy things like a friend's engagement photos and somehow having that convert into the most glaring reminder that you are forever alone and not worthy of happiness. If you already know that your brain does crap like this, simply don't give it as much ammunition to work with right before you go to sleep. Other than that, I encourage you to refer to the things that I wrote in the earlier chapter about good sleep hygiene. Routine is your friend there, too.

We all know the saying: All work and no play sucks hard... or something like that. I totally encourage you to still give yourself the chance to do those little time killers that you love. You should be Netflixing, having a drink, reading your favorite books, and wrecking kids in your video game of choice. The important thing in setting yourself up for success is to be realistic and to be reasonable. Watching a few episodes of a show is great… But do you have the self-control to stop there, or are you the type to fall into an all-day binging marathon if you are left to your own devices? Same goes for all of those other media types that I was talking about. Self-awareness is key. Take a moment to think about your casual activities. Which of these are your personal black holes? Which ones seem innocuous at first, but then suck you in and refuse to let you go until your self-loathing becomes massive enough to satisfy its hunger? If any specific media, hobbies, or pastimes come to mind, that is where you need to watch out.

My personal black hole is gaming. When I decided to give myself a deadline and dive heavily into the writing of this book, I went ahead and uninstalled all of the games from my PC. Is it killing me that I haven't been able to play Fallout 4 yet? Sure, but not nearly as much as it would kill me to miss my deadline and disappoint myself and my fans. My method is a bit drastic, and you probably don't need to go that far. It may be useful for you to impose your own limits though. Set a timer for a reasonable amount of time instead of just waiting until you feel satisfied. Maybe avoid certain activities when you know they represent a high black hole risk and you can't afford to be sucked in at this point in time.

It is also important to consider the effect that these activities have on your mood. What feels satisfying is not necessarily good for your mood. Do you have a sad playlist? Trust me, I understand how satisfying and affirming it can feel to sit next to the window on a rainy day in your frumpiest clothes and listen to Adele while bawling your eyes out. She just *gets* it. As humans, we have an interesting tendency to gravitate toward stuff like that. Every once in awhile, it's okay to do this. Sometimes we just need music to be like that friend who sits with you and pats your back while they acknowledge your misery. Other times we need music to be that friend that tells you to get off your ass and take better care of yourself. I am being specific about music here, but it would serve you well to understand how all different types of recreational activities have an effect on your mood. Sure, your "All the Feels" playlist may be morbidly satisfying when you are already down in the dumps, but does it have a positive effect on your mood? Probably not. Setting yourself up for success sometimes means making the choice to listen to something else instead of driving yourself deeper into that nasty whirlpool of depression.

The same goes for books and games. Many of us have that one story that inevitably whisks us away to another world where we are always welcomed back with open arms. Of course, art of any form has a healthy element of escapism built into it, but does that temporary departure from the real world serve to inspire and motivate you, or does it just make this world seem that much more bleak and meaningless when you come back from your journey? You might be surprised about the way in which these things affect your mood when you take a step back and get really honest with yourself about it.

Look, you are allowed to feel like shit sometimes. You are allowed to dive deep down to the bottom of the well of your own feelings, searching for understanding in the pages of a book, in the flicker of a screen, or in the lyrics of a song. But if you want to kick this depressive state that you are stuck in, you are going to have to be smart about it. That deliciously dramatic misery cannot be the norm. Your depression is like a mold that wants to keep growing until it covers you entirely. If you keep giving it the perfect conditions to grow, it will be very difficult to pull out of that self-sabotaging mode. Use your self-awareness to avoid feeding your depression and instead create the conditions for change and progress.

The classic self-improvement guru Jim Rohn is credited with the popular quote, "You are the average of the five people you spend the most time with." There is most definitely some validity to this idea. We all have friends and family of different varieties. If you really give yourself the chance to think about it, you can probably single out a few people in your life who have a very predictable effect on your mood. The people who have a positive effect are easy to recognize. They are that one friend who always lifts you up and motivates you no matter how much you hate yourself at that particular moment in time. They are that family member who has actually been there before and can relate to you when you talk about the things you're going through. I probably don't need to tell you about the obviously negative ones. You already know them as the people that can make you feel frustrated, pissed off, misunderstood, or guilty, without fail. The answer for those people is probably a bit obvious. If you can spend less time with them for your own sake, it may be the wise choice. Remember those logical barometers that we talked about in the chapter about your thinking patterns? Well, those trusted advisors are also great people to help you determine whether it makes sense to see less of a person or cut ties altogether.

Of course you can't always avoid those people. Sometimes they are your boss, your professor, or your mom. I know it sucks when you can't just cut those people out. It can make you feel even more helpless because it is just one more annoying aspect of your life that you don't have control over. While you may not be in a position to cut these people out of your life entirely, you may still have some control over when you see them and for how long. Much like the tips that I gave about music and other media, I want you to just become more aware of the effect that these people have on your mood. When you are more aware of it, you can plan for it. You can decide when you have it in you to endure some of their bullshit and when you do not. Maybe you need to make sure you follow a visit to your parent's place with a visit to your best friend's, so that they can pick you back up after your parents mopped the floor with your heart. Even when you can't avoid one of these people, knowing the effect that they have on you is valuable in itself. It's kind of like taking a punch or falling while riding a bike. If you know it's coming, you can brace yourself for impact, and it might not wreck you as badly. It will still be shitty, but at least it won't be shitty AND surprising.

Sometimes the people that have a negative impact on your mood are not quite so easy to see. The obvious ones leave you feeling unambiguously bad, while others may have a more subtle effect. How about friends that are always willing to talk to you about what you are going through, but somehow seem to make you feel more annoyed and betrayed by the world when you are finished with your chat? Often, these people have good intentions, but they can't keep their own drama out of the equation and end up magnifying your own negative feelings instead of lifting you up and out of the murkiness. Just like the sad music, sometimes it feels satisfying to be miserable along with someone else, but at least call it what it is. You are not improving your mood, you are scratching that itch for commiseration and validation. Again, you don't need to avoid these people completely, especially if you don't want to. They might be your closest friends or family members that you truly love. Perhaps you just can't emotionally afford to spend a lot of time with them when you are going through this period of progress and positivity. I know it can be tricky to put this sort of reduced contact into action. They might feel irked at you or wonder what they did to piss you off. For this I would refer to the letter that I showed you earlier. I would encourage you to explain to them that you are in a period of progress in which you need to work some crap out, and that this does not always allow you to be emotionally or physically available.

Recognizing the impact that other people have on your mood can take a little practice. I would encourage you to document your experiences in a journal to help you begin to notice some of the more subtle differences that might occur. This method is effective for any activity, not just interaction with other people. The first step is to write down what you are doing at a given time of the day. Next, you rate your mood on a scale from 0 to 10, where 0 is the most miserable you have ever felt and 10 is top of the world awesome. Don't overthink the rating. Think of it as a non-specific overall wellness rating. After you pick out an overall rating that feels right, pick out a few emotion words that seem to fit with how you are feeling. I understand it can sometimes be hard to find the right words to describe how you are feeling, so I will include a list of different feeling words here that you can draw from.

Emotion/Feeling Words (Positive)

- Confident
- Amazed
- Free
- Satisfied
- Lucky
- Thankful
- Festive
- Elated
- Playful

- Optimistic
- Calm
- Comfortable
- Surprised
- Content
- Affectionate
- Warm
- Loved
- Interested

- Curious
- Inspired
- Excited
- Certain
- Secure
- Hopeful
- Entertained
- Wonderful
- Engaged

Emotion/Feeling Words (Negative)

- Angry
- Irritated
- Insulted
- Upset
- Bitter
- Resentful
- Worked up
- Disappointed
- Bored

- Discouraged
- Powerless
- Guilty
- Miserable
- Disgusting
- Uncertain
- Lost
- Embarrassed
- Tired

- Distrustful
- Uneasy
- Tense
- Alone
- Empty
- Vulnerable
- Scared
- Nervous
- Restless

Now that you have documented your baseline emotional state, you can go about business as usual with your friend, family member, acquaintance, or enemy, as the case may be. Once you have transitioned from spending time with that person to the next part of your day, that is where you would repeat the steps from above. If you want to be an overachiever, you can include two additional ratings: one retrospectively regarding how you felt during the time with that person and one a little later to look at the lingering effects that the visit had on your mood. This will likely be difficult to figure out and interpret the first time through. Remember that your brain is being a huge douche by distorting your thinking patterns and tricking you into overgeneralizing. The person in question may indeed have a negative effect on your mood, but in order to have a clear "line" in your data, you will need to gather more information than one single interaction. That means you should complete that tracking process the next few times you see them, and then look back on your collected data as a whole picture and try to make sense of it. When in doubt, ask a trusted advisor or a neutral third party, like a therapist, for their take on it. It might sound a little dumb to "track" your relationships, but you might be really surprised by the sort of power you can derive from becoming more aware of what trends and patterns exist within your interpersonal web. It serves as just one more way that you can take a little control back in your life and exercise that ever important self-awareness to give yourself the best shot at success.

The final tip that I have for you in this section is to always have something to look forward to. Depression has a way of sucking out the hopefulness and future perspective from us. It makes us think about the past which is filled with shittiness, and it makes think of the present, which feels pointless. In the few moments that depression allows us to think about the future, it is typically with the dread of knowing that it is not going to go well. Being in that mode really sucks. The cool thing is that, just like many of the other negative symptoms of depression, you can reprogram your brain into looking forward with excitement to things. I don't mean that you be stoked as hell for every single day of the week, but you can certainly achieve a mild to moderate level of happy anticipation. Basically, we are just looking for enough to pull you through. This is especially important when you are in that zone where every night feels pointless because it seems like tomorrow will be a bland carbon copy of today. Every little bit of motivation or positive anticipation helps to make things feel worth it. These can be simple things. Maybe it is your favorite show on television, an awesome new breakfast spot in your neighborhood, new episodes of a great podcast, or a weekly meetup with one of your friends. The trick is trying to spread out and integrate these awesome little moments into nearly every day of the week. When one gets stale, add in something new.

These are completely personal to you. I don't know your preferences, but here are some of my special moments that pull me through the week: Jeopardy at 7 every night, new episodes of my favorite podcasts at least twice a week, solo coffee shop dates on Friday mornings, television binges with my wife from our giant pile of blankets on the floor of the front room, daily vlogs from my favorite Youtubers, and playing games on my iPad before going to sleep. These are probably completely stupid and boring to you, but they really do help get me through. I am writing this sentence at 11:00 PM on a Tuesday. I am pretty damn tired, and I really don't want to clean the dishes in the sink before going to bed at 12, but I am looking forward to lying in bed and playing some Puzzle and Dragons on the iPad for a few minutes before drifting off, so I have something to look forward to after that boringness of cleaning. Tomorrow, I have to go to the office and do some lame clerical work and psychological assessment scoring, but I know that one of my good friends will probably release a new episode of his podcast that I can listen to while I work. I am sick of doing planks in the morning (seriously, fuck planks), but I know that I can watch Casey Neistat's newest daily vlog on Youtube while I am doing them. I get to walk to work on Thursdays, which is pretty awesome, and I don't have to leave as early as I normally do. And Friday is Friday, which is always cause for celebration.

That gets me through my entire week. It's only Tuesday, but having the entire week punctuated with awesome little moments to look forward to makes me feel like it's almost Friday already.

That basically sums it up for this section. I hope it wasn't too completely random. The takeaway that I want you to remember is: there are so many small (and large) adjustments that you can make to your life to help set yourself up for success. Depression will always be like a cosmic force that drives you to self-sabotage and ruin your chances before you even get the chance to try and be happy. By increasing your self-awareness, collecting data from your life, and being very honest with yourself about the current trends that are playing out, you can instead create the conditions necessary for kicking depression's ass. I doubt that any single adjustment here will be the cure to all of your issues. However, going through this process of fine-tuning these aspects of your life will make it that much easier to make positive, constructive choices for yourself. Every little bit helps. Set yourself up for success.

Ch. 9 Professional Help Is Self-Help

In this chapter, I want to talk about getting outside help from a professional. Ideally, we would all be able to get by on our own. Nifty little resources like this book you are reading would be enough to nudge us in the right direction and get us kicking ass again. Unfortunately, that is not always the case, and we may need a little extra help to get going on our journey. There is absolutely nothing wrong with that. I think that many people have the wrong idea about psychiatric treatment. Getting treatment from a professional does not mean that you have failed at your attempts to help yourself. Self-help is all about making the conscious decision to utilize the tools at your disposal to improve your situation. No one can make change for you. You still have to make that choice to engage with treatment. In that way, I see psychiatric treatment as a sign of strength and as an extension of your own self-help. This tool is available to everyone. It takes a special sort of strength to recognize the need for extra help and to seek it out. (Quick disclaimer: I practice psychology in California, USA. I have little knowledge about how mental health treatment works in other countries, so please be aware that some of the information presented here might not directly translate in your country. The general ideas should still be the same.)

There are two basic categories of psychiatric treatment. By the way... psychiatric is just a catch all term for treatment that deals with psychological or emotional problems. The two broad categories are therapy and medication. You might also hear terms like "counseling", "psychotherapy", or simply "sessions" in place of therapy. We just like to make everything stupidly complicated with a bunch of terms for the same thing. For medication treatment, you might also hear terms like pharmaceutical treatment, psychopharmaceutical treatment, or pharmacological treatment. Again, those all mean the same thing. I am a big fan of both modes of treatment, because I think that they serve different purposes. In general, the types of depression that benefit from medications are of the more physiological type. (You know, that type where you feel like the laziest asshole on earth and your body is screaming at you every time you try to muster up an ounce of energy or motivation.) They can also be helpful as a boost when your therapy and self-help are just not doing the trick and the problem seems to be pretty sticky. When therapy and medication are working in tandem, they can make an exceptionally powerful combo.

I want to explain more to you about these different types of treatment, but before that I should give a disclaimer. Teeeechnically, I am supposed to be an expert about therapy, since that's why I spent a zillion years in school getting my Ph.D. However, I am most certainly not an expert in medication. Later, I will explain the difference between different types of care providers. Just know that I am familiar with medications in my capacity as a therapist, but a medical doctor will be the one that can truly advise (and prescribe) when it comes to psychiatric medications.

So, let's talk about therapy first. Basically, there are two main ways of categorizing types of therapy. The first dimension is what *format* of sessions you are looking at. In other words, are they individual, group, family, or couples sessions? The other dimension is the *type* of therapy that you will be getting. There are many different types of therapy out there that are driven by particular theories about where issues come from and how it is that people can change and improve.

The first type is pretty simple. Individual therapy is probably what you are most familiar with, either from personal experience or from pop culture portrayals of psychological treatment. (Quick side note: television and movies are so goddamn bad at portraying therapy- please don't let them influence your opinions.) Anyway, individual treatment basically looks like one-on-one sessions with a therapist or psychologist.

These sessions are typically 50 minutes long. The "therapeutic hour" is 50 minutes because your shrink needs to write notes on every session for record keeping purposes. Some will write their notes during the session as you speak, and others wait to write them up after you are gone. Either way, they are probably scrambling during the 10 minutes between your session and their next client to wrap up notes, take a drink of water, and pee real quick. The way that these sessions take place can be a bit different depending on the setting. For example, a private practice might be in a small office building or even in a repurposed house. You will likely talk directly with your therapist on the phone or via email to set up your initial appointment. There will probably be either a very small waiting room with at most one or two other people, or there might be no waiting room at all. The picture with larger healthcare systems is a little different. Not worse by any means- just a slightly different experience. I have worked in both settings, and I have found that most people seem to associate the idea of therapy with the private practice setting I described and are sometimes surprised when they find themselves in a healthcare situation that doesn't look all that different from going to the doctor for any other medical reason.

If you are part of a large healthcare system, you will probably talk to the front office staff to schedule your first meeting. Often this first "intake" appointment will be scheduled with whichever clinician is available at a time that works for you. This doesn't necessarily mean that you will stick with that therapist after the first session. Healthcare systems sometimes have people that are specifically employed to conduct initial sessions and then direct you to the most appropriate clinician or other resources that they have available. That said, you can usually expect to see the same therapist for each session once you get the ball rolling. Scheduling can be a little more flexible with private practice, since the therapist is the one who decides what their own business hours and availability are. Appointments in healthcare settings typically need to fall within their business hours, and it can sometimes take a little more negotiating to find a time that you can get an appointment. In this setting, you will probably also be waiting for your appointment in a larger room with other people doing the same thing. If that is concerning for you, just remember that everyone is there for the same reason and values their own privacy. Typically, it's quiet and people are just reading magazines or playing on their phones while they wait. When someone comes into the waiting room to find you for your appointment, they typically won't call your name out loud. Instead, they might ask out loud, "Hello. Is anyone here for Dr. Duff?"

So, let's talk about the first session. In the field we generally call this the intake session, though it can go by any number of names. It all means the same thing. The point of this first appointment is to gather information. It most definitely can be therapeutic and helpful, but it is not going to be the same thing as the routine therapy session that you will have later on. This is a good thing. Sometimes it can be a little frustrating to feel like you are being interviewed when you just want to get some damn help as quick as possible. However, a good therapist should be able to balance hearing you out, gathering information, and being helpful to you in an intake session. The idea is to obtain a solid picture of what you are going through and your personal history. They may be related. You also want to make sure that there is someone there who is a good fit for you. Therapists have different strengths and specialties. Neither of you need to waste too much of your time if for some reason they may not be the best person to help you. If this is the case, it is not your fault, and they can still be helpful by having all of the information that they need to point you in the right direction by making a specific referral to another clinician. In the first session you will go through a diagnostic and historical interview. Basically that means getting your personal story, information about what is currently happening, and trying to develop a working idea about what your potential diagnosis might be. At the end of it, you should be aware of any working diagnoses that are being considered, a greater familiarity with the system that you are working in, and an idea about what the course of treatment might look like.

Courses of treatment can vary. I'd say that the most common interval is weekly appointments. There was a time where session limits were more popular, but treatment is more often open-ended now. Check with your provider, insurance company, or school, as the case may be to find out what their policy is. In my experience, some insurance providers and schools still have loose session limits where there is a required "check in" after a certain number of sessions to see if additional sessions are necessary. If you are still making good use of the support, they generally with not cut you off.

In a typical individual therapy session, you will sit down with your therapist and generally talk about nothing important for a few minutes. This part is important to just ease the tension and transition into a therapeutic environment. You might talk about movies you've seen, the weather, or whatever bullshit pops into your head. After the small talk, they will usually ask you if there are any really important updates that they should know about. Life changes and that sort of thing. From there, it depends on the type of therapy that you are getting. Some modes of therapy will review homework, challenges, assignments, or experiments from the previous session before diving into new content. Others will simply wait for you to speak your mind and follow your lead. What you talk about depends on your particular issues and the theoretical orientation of the therapist. Sometimes, it's a place to just get all of that shit off of your chest that you've been keeping in all week. Friends and family are great, but they biased and there is always some inherent risk to telling them things. With a mental health professional, they will hear you out and be on your team no matter what you tell them. They are there to support you and try to gently guide you on your quest.

The term that we use in the field to describe the opinion that therapists have toward their clients is called "unconditional positive regard." That means that they are always on your side. It does not mean that they will agree with everything you say, but they will not think less of you for saying it. You do not need to worry about scaring them away or making them think you are an idiot for saying the things on your mind. It's an inherently one-sided relationship. That doesn't mean that your therapist will be completely blank and inactive. Not by any means. It just means that you are both there for you. It's different from a friendship, because a therapist should not be pushing their own agenda or looking for you to reciprocate the support. They are there for you because they care and it is their job. Some people make the mistake of feeling guilty, because they come in every week and lay all of this crap on their therapist and feel like the therapist has to just take it without getting anything back in return. While it is true that your shrink is in the business of hearing you out and taking in your thoughts and emotions, they certainly do get something back in return. This is perhaps a bit of a generalization, but most therapists get into the field for a reason. It is inherently rewarding to be able to help other people. As a therapist, you also have the opportunity to learn about such a wide variety of life experiences by having people be so open and honest with you. It's a very uniquely rewarding job, and you don't need to worry about your therapist. Let them worry about helping you become your best self.

At first, it can be a little weird to have a time-limited conversation about your life. Usually when you have these sorts of candid conversations, they are with friends and can go on for any amount of time. In the case of therapy, you will be sticking to a schedule. So usually, you will be hypersensitive to the time for the first few sessions. Eventually, you get the feel for it and it won't feel like a limitation. Most good therapists are able to guide the conversation in a way that fits nicely within the timeline. That means that they will not open up a huge can of worms that causes you to unravel emotionally right at the end of the session. No one wants you to walk out of the room a complete wreck. It can also be a bit awkward to have someone taking notes while you talk. Not all therapists write notes during sessions, but many do. Don't worry about this. It's not like they are making a binding contract based on the words that you have said. More likely they are just jotting down notes to themselves regarding what you said so that they don't have to rely on their memory when going back later to write session notes. Sometimes they also may write down a small note to come back to a topic so that they don't have to interrupt you when you are in the middle of saying something.

For instance, you might be talking about your experience over a holiday and say something like, "It was pretty much what I expected. Everyone came over for dinner and it was just super awkward. John was there, which I definitely did not expect after last year- so that made things worse. I guess it wasn't all bad, though. Dinner tasted great, and I got to see some people in the family that actually seem to understand me. I tried to just hang out with them for most of the night and pretend like the rest of the family wasn't staring at me with judging eyes." During this story, your therapist wouldn't want to interrupt. In order to be fully present in what you are saying, they might just jot down a couple quick notes to come back to such as "John last year?" or "family who understands vs doesn't?" This would allow them come back later and learn more about your experience by asking something like, "I'm glad your holiday wasn't all bad. You did a good job of finding some positive aspects. Do you mind if I ask about something you mentioned in there? Well, you said that there are some people in your family who just seem to 'get it' better than others. What do you think they see or know about you that helps them understand?" It may seem like they are mentally checking out when they are writing something down instead of paying attention to you, but in reality it is probably helping them stay more present in what you are saying.

I talked a bit about individual therapy, so let me talk about some of the other lesser known formats. If you are having relationship issues with your spouse or significant other, you might find yourself in couples therapy. This is different from being in individual therapy and occasionally bringing your significant other in for a session to help round things out. That method of bringing a third person into individual therapy every once in awhile is called having "collateral" sessions. Couples therapy is a bit different, because you are both there from the start, and it's the relationship rather than either of you individually that is being worked on. You will definitely address individual issues as they relate to the relationship, but the "identified patient" is the both of you together. If you are experiencing depression that isn't leading to major difficulties in the relationship, you are probably not going to engage in couples therapy. However, since depression is one of those problems that seems to generate a bullshit vortex and suck other people into it, there is a significant chance that there are also some issues going on in lover-land. If that is the case, it is important to know a few things about couples therapy.

You are allowed to be in individual therapy as well as couples therapy, but probably not with the same therapist. Most good therapists try to avoid the situation where they are more aligned with one partner than the other and will not do couples therapy with someone that they see in individual therapy. Can you imagine being in the therapist's shoes and hearing all of one partner's closest held secrets, fears, and wishes, and then being expected to not let those influence their opinion when seeing both partners at the same time? Not possible. That said, it is pretty common for partners to have individual therapy on their own as well as couples therapy with a separate provider. This way, you can work on the nitty gritty personal stuff in individual therapy and then bring that growth to the table and try to make relationship gains in couples sessions. Just like any therapy format, the way sessions go will be partially dictated by the therapists particular theoretical orientation and approach to treatment. In general, there will be more active strategies employed where you practice skills that will be helpful in your relationship. This might involve practicing different types of communication, expressing concerns in a safe space, or going through exercises in session to address particular issues within the relationship. It's an amazing tool that is available to you. If you are really feeling like you are still in the trenches of depression, it is okay to focus on yourself first, but being open to couples treatment at some point can go a long way toward rectifying some of the damage that may have been done during the rough periods.

Another type of therapy you may have heard of is family therapy. Before you go any further, you should go on Youtube and look up the classic clip from the Simpsons about family therapy. It doesn't have anything to do with what I'm going to say here, but it's hilarious and you deserve a laugh. ANYWAY, family therapy is much like couples therapy in that the "identified patient" typically is the family unit rather than a particular individual. There are many different types of family therapy out there and to be honest, it's not my area of specialty. I can hold my own in family sessions, but that is ALL some people do. I would suggest that you find someone that specializes in family therapy if you are interested in pursuing this avenue of treatment. It should say on their website or their page on therapy search engines whether this is their bread and butter. In general, family therapists think of psychological issues as resulting from problems in the system of a family. That means that your depression isn't just an isolated problem, but it's influenced by other factors within that wonderful group of assholes that you call a family. If you have depression, you probably recognize that family often knows the exact right buttons to push when they want to send you from 0 to 100 on the depression and irritation scale in the blink of an eye. They are also sometimes the exact people you need on your side to beat this thing. In those moments where they look at your eyes you can see a glimmer of understanding and unconditional love, you can feel a trickle of hope drip into your iced over veins. Maybe they can help you get through it.

The actual in-session work is more in line with couples therapy than individual therapy. The therapist will probably have you work on concrete skills and possibly even reenact situations that happened at home to suggest alternative approaches. I won't lie. Family therapy sessions can be tough, especially if your family environment is a place where feelings aren't exactly talked about in the open. The therapist will encourage each member of the family to be present and involved in treatment. Usually when there is some resistance there to start with, that is an indication that you are on the right track. It's like when you really don't want to check your bank account… that's probably the exact time that you need to be checking your balance. To this point, family therapy will often involve a little more introduction and guidance at the start. We don't really expect families to just sit down and "1 2 3 GO!" Instead, the therapist will talk a bit about what to expect from therapy, how they work, and typically guide families as much as needed through those initial stages. It's worth mentioning here that both couples therapy and family therapy also involve intake sessions and are sometimes longer than the standard therapeutic hour to make time for all of the work that needs to be done.

So, let's get back to talking about therapy in general. Just like I have presented you with many different strategies and approaches for fighting back against your depression, therapists that you encounter will have their own particular theoretical orientations that lead to different styles of treatment. A theoretical orientation basically just refers to which school of thought guides your understanding about the source of psychological issues and how they are healed. There are more orientations than I can go into here. Seriously, there are fat textbooks full of them. That said, I want to at least introduce you to a few of the key players.

Probably the most well-known type of therapy is cognitive behavioral therapy, or CBT. You might already be familiar with this approach, especially if you are from the United States. It's definitely one of the more prevalent forms of therapy out there, and for good reason. Its efficacy has been supported through countless important pieces of research. If you have already read through my chapter on adjusting your thinking patterns, you already have a pretty good primer for CBT. The roots of CBT actually come all the way back from stoic philosophy, but you might be more familiar with some of the founding fathers of formal cognitive treatment such as Aaron Beck or Albert Ellis. The cognitive behavioral approach assumes that most psychological issues arise from faulty patterns in our thinking, which can be "unlearned" through a scientific approach to examining our assumptions and automatic responses to situations. A CBT-oriented therapist will help you to identify the patterns in your thinking that get you into trouble to help you stop being such a dick to yourself. They will often engage in something called "collaborative empiricism." That means that you will both put on your scientist hats and dive into your problems together. You will not take your asshole brain at its word. Instead, you will treat the things that it automatically tells you as hypotheses. They are interesting ideas that can either be proven or disproven by examining the evidence. You will work together to find those delicious little nuggets of evidence and apply them to your working hypothesis to see if you really need to be feeling so terrible.

This is definitely one of the more active psychotherapy approaches. There will probably be more structured activities that could involve worksheets or even workbooks so you can develop and internalize a step-by-step process for addressing your unhelpful thinking patterns. Trigger warning: you might even get homework *GASP*. Don't worry, these are not like school homework assignments. They are most likely things like filling out a thought log or doing behavioral experiments in your life. To challenge those negative assumptions that you have. In most cases, CBT will focus less on the past than present issues. The past is considered to be important due to the ways in which it might influence our current patterns of thinking and behavior. For instance, it may be useful to look back at early instances of learning, when you may have been taught that a particular distorted way of thinking was appropriate. You most likely won't focus quite so much on things like deep-seated parental issues or unconscious motivations. I'll offer a word of warning here: CBT is effective, but it can also be a bit challenging. A good therapist will help tailor the treatment to you as a person, but in some cases, old school cognitive therapists can come off as a little harsh. The reason for this is that they're in the business of challenging you and pushing you to not trust your automatic thoughts and instead go where the evidence leads you. This can sometimes be annoying if you don't like to be contradicted or challenged on your thoughts. Even if you have a pretty thin skin, I would still suggest that you give CBT a fair shot. Like I said, most shrinks these days try to be legitimately helpful and find something that works for your particular personality.

Another common type of treatment for those of you that might want to dive a bit deeper and scour your psyche for the roots of your current issues would be psychoanalytic or psychodynamic therapy. I'd be surprised if you haven't heard of Sigmund Freud at this point. He's the grandfather of this approach. If that puts a bad taste in your mouth, just know that we have come a long way since his time. Freud was a brilliant man, but he was also a fuckin' weirdo. The type of therapy that he originated is called psychoanalysis. This is that classic caricature you may have seen in movies or cartoons where someone is lying down on the couch and free associating while the creepy white dude with the pipe and notepad sits silently behind them. There aren't so many therapists who still offer hardcore 3-times-a-week psychoanalysis these days, though they do exist. The more modern version of this (that has a little more structure and a lot more research support) is called psychodynamic treatment. Same roots, just updated to fit with modern times... much more palatable to most people.

In psychodynamic treatment, you will probably look quite a bit more at relationships, especially early relationships that shaped your ways of relating to other people and the world around you. Yes, that probably means Mom and Dad. You will likely dive into all of that stuff that happened during your formative years. That's one of the main distinctions between psychodynamic treatment and more present-focused approaches like CBT. With this type of therapy, there is the assumption that a portion of the iceberg that is your psyche lies beneath the surface. You can expect to work toward uncovering and becoming more aware of subconscious tendencies and wishes that are playing out and influencing your daily life. I consider psychodynamic treatment to be an insight oriented treatment. This means value is placed on uncovering the origins of the issues that are currently causing you so much grief, and there's an assumption that understanding where the issues came from serves as a means to heal and protect.

The actual in-session work will probably be somewhat less structured than CBT. You won't be doing quite as many worksheets or homework assignments, and instead your therapist will be a gentle guide to support you and offer interpretations as you begin to peel back the layers of your psychic onion. A psychodynamic therapist may also draw your attention to patterns that are playing out between the two of you in the moment as a parallel to what goes on in the rest of your life outside of treatment. The idea is that we fall into certain relational patterns that tend to continue in different facets of our life. Many people turn to a psychodynamically oriented interpretation of events when they consider someone in an abusive relationship. For the non-therapist, the most common interpretation of that situation is that they were in an abusive relationship with one of their parents and continue to play out that relationship with other people throughout their life. Don't be turned off by the ancestry of psychodynamic treatment being a little weird. As you can see by that example, it sometimes makes a lot of sense to consider your difficulties through this lens.

Like I said before, those are a couple of the main players in the field of psychotherapy right now, but there are SO many more. You might run into approaches like dialectical behavior therapy, strategic solution-focused therapy, gestalt therapy, family systems therapy, or interpersonal therapy. They all have their unique features and merits. Many modern approaches blend aspects from different theoretical orientations. A therapist that uses an approach that combines several types of treatment is called "integrative", or "eclectic". Sometimes the word eclectic is avoided, just because the connotation in the United States is that an eclectic person is probably strange. Currently, integrated approaches to psychotherapy are more common than pure single-theory approaches and that is perfectly alright. In fact, there is some research that suggests that as therapists practice and become masters of their craft, they naturally begin to drift toward a similar, more integrated approach that combines the most useful aspects from the different theoretical orientations out there.

I definitely fall into the integrated camp. My personal approach to therapy probably lies somewhere between CBT and psychodynamic treatment. I feel that it is important to first stop the "emotional bleeding" in therapy and address what is going on right in the moment. If there is a crisis happening, you can worry about self-exploration later. After the person is stabilized, I use many strategies from CBT and solution-focused therapy to start to help the person develop skills and different ways of thinking that can help them to better interact with their world. Eventually, I believe that it is important to work toward insight and depth of understanding about the origins of problems. To me, I think of this final process as a shield. Sure, you can learn better ways of treating your symptoms and coping, but learning about where they came from in the first place can help you avoid falling into a relapse later on. Theoretical orientation in therapy is basically just the unique way in which your shrink makes sense of your mess. Even if they are going by the book and using whichever techniques are most supported by research for your particular issue, they are probably translating it in their head to make sense with their theoretical orientation.

There are also clinicians that have particular specialties when it comes to the issues that they like to treat. Some therapists prefer to be a jack of all trades type, while others choose to specialize in a particular niche. This is independent of their theoretical approach. For instance, you might have a psychodynamic therapist that specializes in working with survivors of trauma, or you might have a cognitive behavioral therapist that focuses on sexual dysfunction. When you are looking for a therapist, take note about whether they have a specific focus or area of specialty. These concepts of theoretical orientation and area of specialty will be MUCH more important to consider than what school they graduated from when you are searching for a therapist.

Let's shift gears here and talk about how you go about searching for a therapist. (Again, I need to give the caveat that I'm giving advice that is specific to the United States. The process is hopefully similar in other countries, but I've never practiced there, so I can't be sure. Actually, if you don't mind, give me some feedback about that. Tweet me (@duffthepsych) from other countries and help me understand how it is similar or different where you live.)

The way that you search for a therapist will depend on how you plan on paying for it. The main factor to consider is whether you will be using insurance. If you are a university or college student, you probably have access to free or extremely low-cost therapy through your school's insurance plan. In fact, many schools have a clinic right on campus that you can go to. If you want to see whether your school offers mental health services, check out their website. Usually, the student health section of the site is a good place to start looking. Don't be afraid to call or email your school if you need help finding those services. They can sometimes be a little tricky to track down.

If you have private insurance provided by your employer or something like that, you will usually have to search for a therapist that is within your "network." Obviously there are many different types of insurance out there, so this is an inelegant explanation. When in doubt, contact your insurance company directly and ask about it. These days you can usually log into your insurance provider's website and use their own search engine to find mental health providers around you. These tools are great because you can usually filter by different criteria. For instance, you can tell the search engine to find you a female therapist within 10 miles of your zip code that does couples therapy. If you want to kick it old school, you can usually also call and ask for the company to send you a list of all providers near you. These search engines are great for locating therapists, but they often don't do a great job of giving you all of the information that you want. For that reason, I encourage you to visit your potential therapist's website if they have one. This helps to give you a general feel for the person that you might be diving into a therapeutic relationship with. Maybe this is a generational thing, but I have a really hard time deciding to see a shrink if they don't have a website or if their website looks like total shit. Ideally, their site should tell you about them, what sort of treatment they provide, and how to get in contact them to learn more.

If you are using a larger healthcare network for insurance, you may have less of a choice in deciding which therapist you see. Don't be freaked out by this. Usually you will be paired with whoever is available to start with. They want to get you in at a time that works for your schedule to get your into the system and started with your intake appointment. After you have your initial contact and first appointment, they will typically send you to a therapist that can meet your needs. When I say you have less of a choice in the matter, I mean that you won't be able to look at a giant list of people and make your choice out of anyone that seems to be a good fit for you. That does not mean that you don't have choice or influence in who you end up seeing for treatment. You always have a say in the matter. They may suggest a particular therapist for you to start with and you can always switch therapists if need be. You are also allowed to state your preferences. For instance, many survivors of sexual trauma prefer to have a therapist who is not the same gender as their abuser and there is nothing wrong with that. Other people may have preferences in regards to age or interpersonal style. While larger healthcare networks have somewhat less flexibility, you can still work within the bounds of the system to find something that works well for you.

If you don't have insurance or don't want to be constrained by it, you will be looking at paying out of pocket for treatment. The rate for out of pocket therapy sessions can vary quite a bit. For the most part, it is not cheap. It is hard to give a generalized price, but a doctoral level therapist charging their full rate will be in the triple digits per hour. Depending on education level, experience, and specialty, there will obviously be a range in the price here. For some people, price is not a primary consideration and they are willing to pay just about anything within reason for their mental health.

If you can't use insurance and cost is prohibitive (been there...), you will probably want to look for therapists that have a "sliding scale." A sliding scale basically just means that their fee for treatment is adjustable and is dependent on your income (or lack thereof). If you are really hurting in the money department, you can often find treatment for very cheap. This does not mean that you will be getting budget quality therapy.

We are just in the business of helping and don't want you to be without treatment if you really need it. You can find sliding scale therapists individually or as part of regional organizations. To find a therapist in your area that might be able to meet your needs, you can definitely use the all-powerful Google, but that isn't always the most reliable method since a lot of therapists don't focus much on search engine optimization. There is also a really great tool available online through the website of the popular publication Psychology Today. As of right now, the tool is available at therapists.psychologytoday.com, but you know the internet... that url could change in the future. Psychology Today's search engine is a great one because its sole purpose is to help you find a shrink near you. That means it has filters that allow you to search by the issue you are struggling with, type of insurance you have, treatment orientation, religion or faith, and more. It's super nifty. I encourage you to spend a little time just exploring some of the people around you, even if you aren't yet ready to take the plunge and try to schedule something. The last tool that I will mention is that there are often local "psychological associations" that have lists of therapists and other resources in your community. To find these, you can usually just Google the name of your city and psychological association (ex: New York Psychological Association).

It is important to mention your consumer rights as someone who will potentially be getting therapy. One of the main goals of therapy during the early stages is to develop a rapport, or a working relationship, with your therapist. It's just like any other relationship; sometimes you can just tell when you and the other person aren't clicking. Think of it like baristas at the coffee shop. Some of them are great and some of them are shitty. There are also some baristas that make your coffee exactly the way you want it, but can't pull a shot of espresso to save their life. In the same way, there are some shrinks out there are that just legitimately bad at their job and there are others who might be great for some people, but just do not quite float your boat. The bottom line is that therapists are people and we don't always get along super well with every person that we meet. If you are feeling pretty sure that it is not working out with a therapist, you are allowed to move on. Please don't let one negative experience spoil your perception of therapy on the whole. There is a good fit for you out there and by having a "miss", you are actually getting better at recognizing your preferences for a therapist, which you can keep in mind as you continue your search. Therapists should not take it personally. It is part of the job and we understand. They probably felt somewhat of a disconnect as well. Ideally, you would give a therapeutic relationship a little while to develop and see if you can overcome some of these obstacles, but sometimes you really do just know when it's not gonna happen.

Now before I talk about drugs, I want to talk about some of the different names and titles that you might hear in reference to people who provide psychological help. Maybe I should have talked about this before I started throwing the terms around throughout this whole book... oh well.

So, the first thing that we need to make completely clear is the difference between psychologists and psychiatrists. I have no idea why we decided to make these terms so goddamn similar. It's understandably super confusing for anyone that isn't in the mental health field to know the difference. Psychologists are people with a doctoral degree (Ph.D. or Psy.D.) in some form of psychology. They can teach, write, research, practice therapy, or do psychological testing. The one thing that they cannot do is prescribe medication. That is where psychiatrists come in. Psychiatrists are medical doctors (M.D.) that specialize in treating mental disorders through the use of medication. Psychiatrists can do therapy, but they typically do not in this day and age. They will certainly talk to you and be therapeutic in their approach, but the main focus of their job is to gather information, make a diagnosis, and suggest strategies for treatment. So that's the difference between psychologists and psychiatrists. Now that you have that distinction in mind, let me confuse you a little more. You might hear the terms "psychological" or "psychiatric" thrown around as well. When they are not referring to the professions that I just talked about, these terms mean the same freakin' thing. For instance psychiatric illness means the same as psychological dysfunction, which means the same as mental health issues. Just remember that psychiatrists are M.D.s, psychologists are Ph.D.s and that all of the rest basically means the same thing.

In order to practice therapy, one does not have to be a psychologist. At least in the United States, psychologist is a title reserved for those of us with a doctoral degree, but a huge portion of people who provide therapy (which is the same thing as psychotherapy or counseling) do not have doctorates. In other words, not all therapists or mental health clinicians are psychologists. There are definitely regional differences depending on what country you live in, but here we have titles such as Marriage and Family Therapist (MFT), Master's in Social Work (MSW), and Licensed Clinical Social Worker (LCSW), which are master's level graduate degrees that allow someone to practice psychotherapy after going through the state licensure process. You really don't need to worry too much about all of this crap. I just wanted to make sure you had the information in case you come across some of these strange acronyms and wonder what they mean.

When it comes to therapy itself, you are pretty much looking at the same picture regardless of the type of clinician that you see. Someone with a doctoral degree obviously has a few more years of education under their belt and may also specialize in things that master's level therapists cannot do such as teaching at the university level or psychological assessment. That doesn't necessarily mean that they are going to be "better" at therapy than someone with a master's degree. In fact, master's level therapists can be super skilled because they start jumping into clinical practice a lot earlier than doctoral level psychologists and their attention is not as split. By that I mean that in a doctoral program, you are often expected to focus on clinical practice, academic research, pedagogy (teaching), and assessment. On the other hand, someone in an MSW program will be focusing much more exclusively on providing therapy. Really, it comes down to personal preference. There are superstar therapists within any given category.

Okay, so let's talk about drugs now. Yay drugs! This is an area that I am always hesitant to talk about because, as we discussed before, I am not a psychiatrist and medication is not my area of specialty. However, I so often get questions about medication for psychiatric issues that I feel obligated to at least give you my perspective on them as a psychologist. Spoilers: I think that they are incredibly valuable. In my work providing psychotherapy for people, I have had the opportunity to work hand in hand with psychiatrists to develop comprehensive plans that treat both the immediate and the big-picture aspects of psychiatric illness. In my opinion, which is based on both clinical research and my own experience, the best course when considering psychopharmacological (drug) treatment for depression is to combine it with therapy. Both therapy and medication are effective, but for that sticky, gross, oppressive kind of depression that some of you are experiencing, the most effective thing is combining medication and solid psychotherapy. The reason for this is that they treat the problem from different sides.

Remember how I mentioned earlier that sometimes fighting against your depression is so hard because you are literally fighting against your biology? Well, psychiatric medications can help with that by temporarily modifying your biology so that it is less of a roadblock on your quest to improve. If your symptoms are so oppressive that it is hard for you to make any changes to your thinking or progress in therapy, that is when you may want to consider medication. Most people are a bit wary of medication, which is a good thing.

You don't want to rely on it as a first line defense for depression. Let's return to that backpack metaphor we talked about at the beginning of the book. If having depression is like walking through your life with a backpack full of bricks weighing you down, medication serves the purpose of taking out a few of those bricks for you. It doesn't solve any direct problems for you, but it frees you up to be less of a slave to your symptoms so that you can make positive changes to your thinking patterns, your behaviors, your environment, and all of that good stuff. Of course, there are individual differences in this, but it is typically nobody's goal to keep you on antidepressant medication for your entire life. If I can throw another metaphor here, you can think of medication as providing you with an initial boost or elevation. Ideally, you take advantage of that boost to build the skills that you need, either through self-help or through therapy, to create scaffolding underneath you. That way, when the support of the medications is eventually phased out, you still have this structure that you have built through all of your hard work that will keep you elevated and you won't tumble back down into the nasty black pit of depression.

The way that antidepressant medication works is related to those neurotransmitters that we talked about during the motivation chapter. There are many different types of medication that are effective for treating depression. Each type has a different mechanism of action by which they alter your biology and help to take that immense weight off of your chest. You really don't need to know about all of them. Leave that to your psychiatrist. Currently, you are probably most likely to run into a class of medications called SSRIs, or selective serotonin reuptake inhibitors (catchy right?). Let me break that down to make a little more sense. So, you have those neurons right? They are the cells in your brain that communicate with one another by sending neurotransmitters back and forth. When neuron #1 sends a neurotransmitter across the synapse (space between neurons) to neuron #2, neuron #2 needs to have a receptor open to receive that neurotransmitter. If it does not, the neurotransmitter continues to bounce around in the synapse looking for a home. We don't want a bunch of homeless neurotransmitters bouncing around in there though, so the brain has a nifty function called reuptake. If the neurotransmitter does not find a home in neuron #2, after it bounces around for a while, neuron 1 will reuptake the neurotransmitter because it doesn't appear to be necessary. So when you want to have MORE of a certain neurotransmitter available, the obvious solution would be to increase the amount of that neurotransmitter that neuron #1 pumps out. A more elegant solution, which is what SSRIs do, is to prevent the reuptake of the neurotransmitter. If there is a lot of the neurotransmitter floating around in the synapse, there is a higher chance that any open slot on neuron #2 will be filled quickly. So, that's about the simplest way that I can break down the way SSRIs work. Instead of letting neuron #1 suck back up the unused serotonin in the synapse, SSRIs tell it to just let them be homeless for a while in the hopes that eventually there will be some space for them in neuron #2. You can also think about it in terms of that pub metaphor that we used earlier. Let's say the neuron #1 is sending patrons to the pub at neuron #2. If some people can't get into the pub because it's full, they will likely wander around and look for another pub. Typically neuron #1 will say, "Hey guys, sorry for the bad suggestion. Come back over here, so you don't have to wait out in the cold." Inhibiting reuptake would mean that the patrons have no other option except to wait in line for the pub at neuron #2 because neuron #1 isn't opening its doors to let them back in. As any good bar or club manager knows, a long line is a good thing. That means steady service. In the same way, a bunch of neurotransmitter floating around in the synapse means a more steady effect. Got it? Good.

Here's something that I really, really want you to understand about antidepressants. With very few exceptions, **they do not start working immediately.** In general, most antidepressant medications take about three or four weeks to alter your brain biology and give you that sweet relief that you are looking for. You need to take my word for this. A lot of people make the mistake of stopping medication because they feel like it "isn't working". Don't be that person! I know that it can really suck to not feel a sudden jolt of relief when you take the medication, but if you stick with it, the relief will come. The other kind of shitty thing about medication is that they can have side effects. As I mentioned before, there is no such thing as a biochemical free lunch. If you are altering your biology, you can have some unintended effects. For antidepressants the common ones are: dry mouth, weight gain, decreased sexual desire, or difficulty reaching orgasm. Obviously these suck. Getting fat and crappy in the sack is not going to help with the depression. However, it is important to realize that not everyone has side effects. Furthermore, if you have side effects from one medication, there is still a good chance that you won't have the same side effects from a different medication. It's a cost-benefit analysis. In a perfect world, you would not need medication to help, but since you may need that extra boost to help you kick depression's ass, you need to be the one to judge whether any the benefits outweigh the potential costs.

I hope this gives you a somewhat better idea about what psychiatric medication is all about. I barely scratched the surface here. There are many different types of antidepressant medication. There are also medications that serve as "mood stabilizers" for people that are dealing with bipolar symptoms. Just like my advice regarding therapy, don't give up if a medication does not seem to be working for you. Talk to your psychiatrist about it. Everyone has slightly different brain chemistry. Though we are getting closer, we don't currently have the perfect blood test to tell you the perfect medication for your particular form of depression. Sometimes, a little bit of trial and error is necessary to dial in the right treatment for you. (Yet another reason that you should engage in therapy in tandem with medication.) Therapy *does* start to make change quickly. Work at this thing from multiple angles and you will prosper. If I might offer a final piece of advice related to medication here, please try your best to see a psychiatrist about it. Your primary care doctor can typically prescribe you psychological medication if you ask for it, but it is important to realize that they do not specialize in that type of treatment. They are not as trained to recognize the nuances involved in psychopharmacological treatment. A psychiatrist has a broader knowledge about the subject and is more readily able to provide you with an accurate diagnosis before moving forward with treatment. Okay. Stepping off of my soapbox now.

I think that about covers it for the treatment section of this book. I know that I didn't go into excruciating detail about every single topic, and that is intentional. I just want you to have a better understanding of what additional value professional help might be able to provide in your quest. By no means is this something that every single one of you needs to follow through with, but I hope this clears up some of the nonsense. Don't be afraid to reach out. If you need help in taking the first step toward professional help, ask someone that you trust to give you a hand. If you need someone to take you to your first session because you are too scared to go by yourself, make that happen. Whatever it takes. This is your health we are talking about here. You have the capacity to dig your way out of this and one of the skills that will help you along the way is being able to recognize the best tools that you have at your disposal. Now you have another depression-crushing tool in your Batman-style utility belt should you need it.

Ch. 10 Adventure Time

Maybe you haven't picked up on this yet, but I can sometimes be a huge nerd. For better or for worse, I was basically raised by video games and the Internet. The downside of this is that I have probably shaved a few years off of my life by spending way too many sleepless nights with abysmal nutrition, binging on whatever game had ensnared my soul at the time. The plus side is that in my own life, I have been able to overcome some pretty significant obstacles and achieve my goals by reimagining my life through the lens of a game. It's not necessarily a new concept. You have probably heard the term "gamification" before, which basically means integrating elements from game design to make something more engaging, motivating, and fun. Brands and products are no strangers to the idea of making things more game like. Take the Starbucks app as an example. You essentially gain levels by spending more money and time at Starbucks, which in turn unlocks different upgrades and status levels. Humans fucking love games. Why do you think Vegas works? It's not like that place would still be standing if people actually tended to win money. Gamification is not all about conditioning you to spend more money on greedy brands though. It is a topic that is actually getting a lot of traction in the scientific literature as a way to promote physical and mental wellbeing. What I want to talk about here is one of approximately five zillions ways that you can integrate elements of game design into your life to amp up the already amazing efforts that you are putting forward in your fight against depression. I must mention that, while gamification is broadly supported in the scientific literature for a variety of issues, my particular flavor and spin on it has not been studied. That doesn't mean that it won't work for you... I just can't *promise* you that it will. If you are interested in seeing an amazing example of gamification that has been *proven* to work, I encourage you to check out the work on the amazing Dr. Jane McGonigal. She crafted an entire game, program, app, and book that stemmed from her experience in recovering from a traumatic brain injury. For someone that really lives and breathes this stuff, look into her book <u>Super Better</u>.

Okay. Enough of me kissing other people's asses. This is my book after all. The first step in any game is to define the heroes and villains. If you've ever played the old school Pokémon games, you know what I'm talking about. You know at the beginning of the game after you mash the A button over and over to get through the first few paragraphs of dialogue, and then some stupid twerp comes walking into the frame saying something witty and acting all smug? That's when you get the prompt to painstakingly select one letter at a time to spell out your own character's name and give your nemesis a moniker as well. If you're like me, you probably made your rival's name something clever like your best friend's name or the name of your worst teacher at the time. Now, I know you are not exactly at the start of your quest to defeat depression, but there is no time like the present to put a name to the bastard. I'm serious. Name your depression. Anything you want. It can be something straightforward like Ned or Dolores, or it can be something snazzy like Sucklord or DepressoTron9000. Pick a name that resonates with you. Imagine yourself saying, "Man. I kicked _____'s ass today!" Personally, I am partial to the funny names. When you are having a bad day, telling yourself that your depression is acting up just doesn't have the same umph as saying Sucklord is acting like a douchecanoe. See? I'm cracking up just thinking about it. Really visualize this. I want you to imagine a battle scene in your head where you are standing on one side and your evil nemesis is standing on the other. You guys are about to throw down in a fight of epic proportions.

OH WAIT. We haven't picked your name yet! "But what do you mean, Robert?? I already have a name." Well sure... you have your normal, plain IRL name. What about your hero name? If you want to keep the same name, more power to ya! You don't have to though. This name is for you alone. Will you be Sally the Suckitude Slayer? TheSmileBomber? Maybe it's just a normal name that you think fits your depression destroying alter ego a little better. For some reason when I was a little kid, I always thought Chad was the coolest name. Chad was the dude that had a chain wallet and talked back to his parents. So cool. Whatever name sticks out to you is perfect. You can even change it as you go on. This is your alter ego in this quest. You don't need to share it with anyone else unless you feel like you want to. Maybe it's a name that evolves over time as you make progress and "level up" your character by going through different real life experiences. The DC Comics character Oliver Queen is getting lots of airtime at the moment through the television show "Arrow." In that story, he starts off branded as "The Hood" or "The Vigilante" when he has one particular agenda to seek justice at any means necessary. Then he becomes "The Arrow" when he tries to turn a new leaf and stop killing people all the time. Eventually, he adopts the moniker "The Green Arrow" when he decides to become the hero that the city deserves. Maybe your name evolves along with you. Either way, don't stress about it. This is about how you feel right now and who you want to be as you move forward on this journey.

Awesome. You're off to a good start. Now you have the key players in your game. It's time to define some of the other parameters. Any good game consists of a series of different tasks that allow you to progress in some way. Not unlike life, eh? Often you have main storyline quests that drive the narrative forward and serve as the ultimate goals for you to achieve. These main quests are broken up into side quests that you need to accomplish along the way. In the search for the Holy Grail, one does not simply encounter it on a leisurely stroll one fine afternoon. Obviously, there are people to talk to, monsters to slay, and journeys to be had before you can get to that point.

It is important to recognize what the main quests are in your story. When you take a moment to think about it, you might be surprised to realize that you have been so caught up in the moment-to-moment grind of simply surviving your depression that you aren't exactly sure what your ultimate goals are. This is your next task. Get out a sheet of paper, start a new doc, or do whatever works for you and start writing down your main quests. Don't be shy here. Being able to maintain a romantic relationship without depression interfering may be a huge epic quest that you are nowhere close to at the moment, but that is exactly the thing that you should be writing down here. These are your big goals. Things that seem simple to other people, but nearly impossible to you. Obviously, you will need to come up with your own main quests, but here are a few potential examples: transitioning off of antidepressant medications, holding a job without being fired or quitting for an entire year, finding a healthy long term relationship, being able to look at yourself and feel proud instead of disgusted, or even something more specific like running a marathon. As always, there are no wrong answers here, and you are free to modify and tweak these as you continue forward. In your journey, these are your grails. In time, you will achieve them, but there will most certainly be some steps to take along the way. That brings you to your next task.

Now that you have a nice list of your epic final quests, it is time to break them down into side quests. These should be things that you need to accomplish along the way to your final goals. In the gaming world, these are tasks such as slaying a minor foe blocking the path to your final destination, fetching some relic from a faraway land that will imbue you with new strength and powers, or gathering materials to construct a stronger weapon. They should still be a bit difficult and take work, but they should be smaller, more attainable quests that you can conceivably get started on now. For example, if one of your main quests is to have a stable job for a year, there are definitely a few steps that would have to come before that.

Obviously, you need to get a job before you can start worrying about keeping it over an extended period of time. So what do you need to get a job? Well, you will need to apply, interview, and agree to some sort of contract or work agreement. Each of these elements will be comprised of other small tasks, such as picking up and filling out applications, writing a resume if applicable, getting appropriate clothing for the interview process, and following through with interviews when offered. So, you can see here how the main quest of keeping a job for a year breaks down into several side quests that must be completed along the way. While it is always wise to break complex undertakings into smaller parts, using the frame of a game certainly helps me wrap my mind around the ways I might need to deconstruct my larger goals into more manageable pieces.

Another aspect of games that makes them so addictive is the process of getting better and better. Most games represent this progress through "leveling up." For instance, most role playing games give you an overall level and also allow you to increase the level of different skills and attributes. This gives you many micro-level progressions to focus on. There is a game called Diablo 2 on the computer that I played for many years when I was younger. The final goal in that game is to defeat the ultimate boss, Diablo (or Baal in the expansion). If that was the only goal of the game, it would be really boring, but the beauty of the game is that they reward you for playing from the first few moments. Let's say I decided on the sorceress character, because I wanted to slay the hordes of demons and undead with vicious arcane spell craft. I start the game as a level one sorceress, but soon after I leave town and begin defeating enemies, I level up. Awesome! That means I get to decide what skill I want to invest in. Let's put a level into firebolt, so I can keep my distance and set some bastards ablaze. I also get 5 points to spend on my attribute points. Do I dump them into vitality so I can have more life force and take more hits? Maybe I should put them into energy so that I can cast my shiny new

139

firebolt skill more often. See what's going on here? I have barely played the game for 5 minutes and I've already been given a bunch of micro-choices and micro-rewards. You can apply this same concept to your self-help quest.

I want you to think about the various skills and attributes that are integral to your own personal depression journey. Skills would be tools like the things we have talked about in other chapters of this book. For instance, the thought log that we mentioned. That is a skill that totally fits into this conceptualization. The first time you encounter with a foe in the form of some negative thinking patterns, you will probably get your ass handed to you because your skills aren't that strong. Maybe you remember reading about how writing down your thoughts can help, but you can't quite recall the method and the different distorted thinking patterns that you were supposed to identify. That's okay; you give it your best shot and work toward improving that skill. Once you level up your thought log skill a bit, you can be more confident as you tackle situations that have potential to send you into a depressive spiral. Other skills to level up might be deep breathing, mindfulness, or even physical abilities like running or using the squat rack at the gym. There are different schools of thought when it comes to levelling up skills. Sometimes, it is most useful to try to level up all of your skills equally, so that you have a well-rounded toolkit to draw from. There may be other instances where investing heavily into one skill will help you most in your particular situation. Maybe you have nothing to worry about when it comes to physiological issues, but you find yourself consistently crushed by guilt, procrastination, and distractions. That would indicate that you don't need to level up physical skills much. Instead, you should probably dump as many points as possible into mindfulness so that you can better take things in stride and build up some resistance to getting thrown off track by negativity.

That brings us to attributes. These are slightly different than skills. I will use a physical example again because it is easy to understand. In the previous paragraph I talked about running as a skill that you could focus on leveling up. However, leveling up your running skill is going to be somewhat difficult until you invest some points into your cardio attribute. See what I did there? The attributes are the underlying aspects of yourself that provide the backbone for building your skills and working toward completion of your quests. Remember the job example? If you dove in at level one and tried to snag a great job, you might have a hard time because you are missing out on some attributes. Confidence, charisma, verbal and written communication, and motivation are all attributes that underlie that particular quest. You will probably want to level those up a bit to make the process easier for you. There are many different attributes that could be areas of focus for you. You will need to decide those for yourself by breaking down your goals step by step like we have been. Break up your main quests into side quests, ask yourself what skills you will need to accomplish those side quests, and then consider which attributes underlie those abilities. Some of these attributes may have a very clear method of leveling up. For verbal communication, you can practice interview questions with a friend. That's pretty straight forward. You practice your verbal communication more, you 'll level up that attribute. Confidence is one that might be a bit more abstract. For attributes like that, you can certainly find your own ways to train them, but will often find that you are leveling them up as you continue that natural process of bettering yourself as you pursue your quests.

Leveling up and progressing as a character is pretty motivating on its own, but no game would be complete without some rewards, right? Every hero deserves some awesome loot. When you defeat the boss battle, the best part is walking past their limp body to go open up the chest that is radiating golden light in every direction. When you find an amazing item in that chest, it makes you want to just jump back into questing to find more stuff. In real life, rewards are not always built into the process. That doesn't mean that you should not have your epic loot to go along with your rising character level and list of completed quests. You just have to make your own rewards. There is this concept in the field of psychology (and animal training for that matter) called operant conditioning. Basically, it just means that if you reward a behavior, the subject will be more likely to do it more often, and if you do not reward it, their rate of the behavior will decrease. There is nothing wrong with rewarding yourself for a job well done. It's science! Use your indulgences and treats to keep you motivated and happy along the way.

The trick is finding rewards that are consistent with the difficulty level of the quest. A small side quest, such as writing down an outline of your activities for the next day, probably lends itself to a minor reward like a scoop ice cream or 15 minutes of your favorite mobile game. On the other hand, finishing your final project at school or finally asking someone out on a date might be more worthy of a moderate sized reward like dinner at your favorite restaurant or that sweater you have been eyeballing in the window at the mall. Your final bosses and epic quests should have epic sized rewards. Taking part in a modeling competition when you were previously too embarrassed to even show your bare arms is a huge deal and should be rewarded thusly. Maybe it's time to cash in some vacation days or finally buy yourself the new game console that you've been wanting.

Of course, these do not have to be money dependent. If you are low in the funds department, get creative with your rewards. Time is the most valuable currency you have, and sometimes taking an entire day off to spend however you would like is just as awesome as buying something. We can't pretend that money is not a factor, though. In some ways it makes the effect even stronger if money isn't exactly coming out of your ears. If you wanted to assign an epic sized reward to one of your main quests, you will probably have some time to save toward it. Put money away each month for your prize. Make a physical or virtual piggy bank, and start building up to your gadget, vacation, experience, etc. That way, you not only have the satisfaction of demolishing your quest to look forward to, but also the epic loot that has been waiting for you throughout your entire journey. Trust me, it will feel SO damn good to open up that chest. I can't freaking wait to buy myself a new Playstation or Xbox when I finally release this book. Even when the intrinsic motivation of helping people and bolstering my income is falling short, the promise of some sweet, sweet gaming time pulls me through!

Now it's time to put all of these pieces together. Remember that this is just one of many different ways you can gamify the process of self-improvement. My version of gamification is particularly nerdy and is mainly influenced by role playing games such as Diablo, Fallout, D&D, and Elder Scrolls, so I'm going to keep running with that here. However, that does not have to be the case for you. I encourage you to take everything that I am saying as inspiration and as a jumping off point. You can convert this into some form that really makes sense to you, given your unique interests. Anyway, the way that I like to wrap this all together neatly is to make a character sheet. These really have their origins back in old school Dungeons and Dragons, where you would have a sheet of paper that you would write down all of your character's information, attributes, and skills. Just do a Google search of "D&D character sheet" if you want to see what I mean. I will include a small version of a character sheet here that you can also print off by visiting duffthepsych.com/bookresources.

CHARACTER SHEET

DRAWING	NAME:
	LEVEL:
	LOCATION:
	RIVAL:

QUESTS

		SKILLS	LEVEL
MAIN QUEST:			
SIDE QUEST:		1.	
SIDE QUEST:		2.	
SIDE QUEST:		3.	
MAIN QUEST:		4.	
SIDE QUEST:		5.	
SIDE QUEST:		ATTRIBUTES	LEVEL
SIDE QUEST:		1.	
MAIN QUEST:		2.	
SIDE QUEST:		3.	
SIDE QUEST:		4.	
SIDE QUEST:		5.	

This is where you get to go through and insert all of the things that we went through in this chapter. Write down your character name and the name of your rival, and draw a picture! You can make it realistic or a projection of the badass that you want to be. No one else has to see this, so it doesn't matter if you are a good artist or not. You could even insert a picture of a popular character that you would like to draw inspiration from. Have fun with it. Then you will want to determine your final quests. These are the big picture ones that we talked about. You can choose as many or as few as you would like, and it's okay to change these as you go along. Treat this like a snapshot that you can always come back to and adjust. Underneath each final quest, you will then break it up into smaller side quests that should be completed on your way to those larger goals. In a separate area, I want you to consider those skills and attributes that we talked about. Looking at your main and side quests, which five main skills and attributes are going to be most important?

CHARACTER SHEET

DRAWING	NAME: Duff
	LEVEL: 1
	LOCATION: Middle Earth
	RIVAL: Prof. Suckitude

QUESTS

	SKILLS	LEVEL
MAIN QUEST: Get a job		
SIDE QUEST: Finish application	1. Thought log	2
SIDE QUEST: Get interview clothes	2. Mindfulness	2
SIDE QUEST: Practice questions	3. Exercise technique	1
MAIN QUEST: Feel physically healthy	4. Scheduling	3
SIDE QUEST: Lose 10 pounds	5. Journaling	3
SIDE QUEST: Develop meal plan	ATTRIBUTES	LEVEL
SIDE QUEST: Find workout buddy	1. Motivation	1
MAIN QUEST: Find a relationship	2. Confidence	2
SIDE QUEST: Sign up for online profile	3. Passion	4
SIDE QUEST: Ask for contact info	4. Physical stamina	2
SIDE QUEST: Go on a date	5. Helpfulness	3

There you have it. You can assign different rewards to your quests and update your levels as you progress. Maybe you will be the type to grind levels intensively for the next few weeks here while you practice your skills nonstop, or maybe you will take things slower and level gradually as you chip away at your quest log. Whatever works for you is exactly what you should be doing. Get pumped about this. Instead of looking at your life as something that has fallen too far into the shitty abyss of depression, think of it as an epic adventure game. Everyone has to start from level one. In no time, you will begin to see progress, and you will feel the excitement build as you get stronger and stronger. Next thing you know, you will be ready for the final battle with your arch nemesis. You can do this thing. Go forth and be the amazing adventurer that you are.

Thank you!

Hey you did it! Hell yeah! You made it through the book. I'm super proud of you. Don't underestimate how big of a deal this is. Even if this book wasn't everything that you were looking for and more... you still did it. You, the person seeking out resources to help them with depression, decided to make some moves and read an entire book about depression. You're already doing it, my friend. Nice work.

I want to say thank you from the bottom of my heart for reading this book. The world is full of a gajillion different resources meant to help you tackle depression. For some reason, you decided to pick up a book that says "fuck" in the title. That makes you awesome. Thank you for taking the chance on this book. I really hope that it made a difference for you in some way.

If I could ask a favor... please consider leaving me a review for this book on Amazon. Not only does it help more people see this book, but it helps people to understand *why* they should get the book. It takes just a couple minutes and it makes a world of difference. Head over to Amazon and tell the world why you did or did not love the book. Whether it is a 5-star or a 1-star review, I greatly appreciate your time and willingness to help me out.

If you are interested in taking your experience with Hardcore Self Help beyond the page, you can follow me on Twitter @duffthepsych, you can like the Duff The Psych Facebook page or you can join our private subreddit at reddit.com/r/hardcoreselfhelp. All you need to do for the subreddit is to go to that url, sign in, and "message the moderators" to request access. That is a place where you can talk to other people on the same journey. You can share your triumphs and ask for support.

Finally, if you want to share feedback with me directly, you are more than welcome to email me. Just shoot a letter over to duffthepsych@gmail.com with the subject line: feedback. I read them all and I try to respond to as many as I can. I'm always open to constructive feedback and I am always stoked to hear about how the book may have helped you personally.

That's it, folks. Gimme a high five, or fist bump, or whatever you kids do these days!